BETWEEN A MAN AND A WOMAN?

LUDGER H. VIEFHUES-BAILEY

BETWEEN A MAN AND A WOMAN?

WHY CONSERVATIVES
OPPOSE SAME-SEX MARRIAGE

COLUMBIA UNIVERSITY PRESS *New York*

Columbia University Press
Publishers Since 1893
New York   Chichester, West Sussex
Copyright © 2010 Columbia University Press

Library of Congress Cataloging-in-Publication Data
Viefhues-Bailey, Ludger H., 1965–

Between a man and a woman? : why conservatives oppose same-sex
marriage / Ludger H. Viefhues-Bailey.

p. cm. — (Gender, theory, and religion)
Includes bibliographical references and index.
ISBN 978-0-231-15620-2 (cloth : alk. paper) — ISBN 978-0-231-52101-7
(ebook)

1. Same-sex marriage—Religious aspects—Christianity.   2. Christian
conservatism—United States.   3. Same-sex marriage—United States.
4. Focus on the Family (Organization)   I. Title.   II. Series.
BT707.6.V54 2010
261.8'35848—dc22

2010009995

∞

Columbia University Press books are printed on permanent
and durable acid-free paper.
This book is printed on paper with recycled content.
Printed in the United States of America

c 10 9 8 7 6 5 4 3 2 1

References to Internet Web sites (URLs) were accurate
at the time of writing. Neither the author nor
Columbia University Press is responsible for URLs
that may have expired or changed since the manuscript was prepared.

For Kevin Jerome Bailey

CONTENTS

CONTENTS

AUTHOR'S NOTE

Making sense of conservative Christian opposition to same-sex love is a project that has more than just academic ramifications. As a scholar of religion, I am interested in examining how religious, national, and sexual concerns intertwine in conservative Christian discourses about homosexuality. Analyzing these interrelations correctly, I believe, will further our understanding of how religious practices shape and are shaped by secular polities, in the United States and beyond. Many times when I report on my work in academic settings or in private, people share with me their personal experiences: A young gay man describes growing up in a conservative Christian household, and an evangelical minister talks about how he loves his lesbian daughter but cannot endorse her "lifestyle." Stories such as these give a glimpse into the conflict-laden biographies that are entangled in how conservative Christians talk about same-sex love—in the streams of words, narratives, and images that circulate among them and that they use to converse with a wider public.

A closer look at these stories shows how words can fail. For example, the Christian minister who feels compelled to tell "God's truth" to his beloved daughter knows that doing so will alienate her profoundly. Yet despite his awareness that his words of biblical truth and compassion cannot reach her, he cannot name the love that his child and her life partner share. Words fail him. Consequently, silences and superficial chatter mark his family's gatherings, which only now and then are interspersed by outbursts of potentially meaningful conversations that lead nowhere. The languages of biblical truth and love that are supposed to be life giving threaten to undermine his family. At the same time the languages circulating among many political analysts fail as well. It is not sufficient to explain conservative Christian resistance to same-sex love simply as the result of bigotry or a politically motivated ploy to galvanize Republican core voters. These kinds of "explanations" do not account for the complexities of convictions that hinder men such as the minister from acknowledging that gay and lesbian Americans are bound to each other by love.

Perhaps it is for biographical reasons that I want to give more attention to the theological plight expressed by conservative Christian language about same-sex love, and perhaps it is for biographical reasons that I want to probe more deeply into the webs of meanings it spins. Thus, I must admit that as a gay man and as someone who, before turning to the more sanguine profession of religious studies, spent a decade engaged in Christian ministry, I am reticent to take the diagnosis of bigotry or political motives as the full story. Obviously, I do not consider it to be theologically problematic that I love another man (particularly the one to whom I dedicate this book). On the contrary, as I have argued in another context, such love is religiously productive. And others, such as orthodox rabbi Steven Greenberg and Christian theologians Eugene Rogers and Mark Jordan, have given profound and nuanced accounts of the religious fruits of same-sex love.[1] However, I have spent many years in a Christian world that is not welcoming and affirming to homosexuals and know that religious arguments and narratives are not easily discounted. Therefore, although this book is not a piece of theology, I want to treat carefully the conservative Christian language under review by neither claiming to understand it too quickly nor declaring it to be incomprehensible.

Philosopher Ludwig Wittgenstein was particularly concerned about conversations that bring our words to the point of failure—as in the case of the minister, when they seem to produce clarity but create confusion, or as in the case of much political commentary, when our explanations obscure the fact that we do not understand what is going on. In these cases, the incessant repetition of cherished positions ("The Bible tells me that homo-sexuality is a sin" or "They reject same-sex love because they are biblical fundamentalist bigots") obscures more than it enlightens. For Wittgen-stein, these are situations where we have replaced a quest for mutual intel-ligibility with sloganeering. At this point, it is important to stop the flow of words and to reflect on what we are saying or what we want to say—to ex-amine the reach and underground of our words, narratives, and images. In short, instead of slogans we need new attempts at understanding both our own words and those of our opponents.

Not everyone may think that understanding, making myself understood, or being understandable is a value in a democratic society. It certainly is not an absolute value. Yet the perils of abdicating public intelligibility are clear, particularly now that there seems to be some movement in the political de-bates about same-sex marriage. Refusing to understand a person's words (even if they seem difficult to comprehend) implies a refusal not only to be in communication but also to be in a shared political space with him or her. Here I concur with Wittgenstein's conviction that when sloganeering is rampant we need to take special care for the contours of our language. Thus, although this book is mainly an academic text, I hope that its goal of under-standing will also engage those of us who, as listeners or speakers, wrestle with conservative Christian language about same-sex love.

ACKNOWLEDGMENTS

This book would not have appeared without the encouragement and critique of many scholars to whom I am very grateful. Among them are Stanley Cavell, Sarah Coakley, Shannon Craigo-Snell, Rebecca L. Davis, Stephen Davis, Siobhan Garrigan, Mark Jordan, Jonathan Katz, Kevin O'Neil, Eugene Rogers, and Graham Ward. Moreover, my work would not be what it is without the experience of teaching insightful and enthusiastic students. I am particularly grateful for the graduate and undergraduate students who, together with my colleagues, make the Department of Religious Studies at Yale University an intellectually stimulating place. Part of the research for this book was generously supported by the Fund for Lesbian and Gay Studies at Yale and thus by those who contribute to the well-being of this fund and university. I would like to thank them, as well as my editor at Columbia University Press, Wendy Lochner, my copyeditor Carol Anne Peschke, and Professor Amy Hollywood, who graciously offered this book a place in the Gender, Theory, and Religion series.

BETWEEN A MAN AND A WOMAN?

INTRODUCTION

Religious language is ubiquitous in the arguments against social acceptance or even legal protection for gays and lesbians. Historically, only a few ministries or gay and lesbian rights groups drew explicitly on religiously motivated ideas of justice; mostly, however, religious language was used to defend a legal and social status quo in which gays and lesbians were subjected to various degrees of discrimination.[1] Today a handful of mainstream denominations endorse the idea that a loving relationship between adults of the same sex is religiously acceptable. Yet the most vociferous resistance against such love still comes from religious organizations and persistently uses religious language. This prolonged and adamant religious resistance demands the labor of understanding. What is religiously at stake, when it comes to the love of same-sex couples? And how can we, as a multireligious public, evaluate these particular religious concerns that fuel an ongoing public policy debate?

This book addresses these questions by examining how conservative Christian organizations, particularly the media, advice, and ministry group Focus on the Family (abbreviated as Focus herein), talk about gays and lesbians. I will argue that the conservative Christian visions of sexuality implicated in our policy debates express what Christian theologians would call a corporeal theology of grace, meaning a reflection on how to negotiate in our sexual bodies the relationship between God's power and human power in the drama of salvation. This theology of divine power links up with American ideals of sexuality and political stability. Analyzing the contemporary debates about gay and lesbian love shows how American sexual and theological visions coalesce in forming strategies to distribute political power.

Perhaps surprisingly, not a doctrinal belief in the inerrancy of the Bible but a wider web of religious and political interests supports this American sexual and political theology. Thus, I do not take the statement "The Bible tells Christians to reject homosexuality as sinful" as the endpoint of a conversation. Rather, I will treat it as the beginning of an inquiry into the intertwining of religious, sexual, and political discourses. Ideas about the character of God's love and power, claims about the allegedly natural aggression of men, the receptivity of the ideal Christian, and the trope of female submission, the defense of heterosexuality from the onslaught of sexual couplings of ill repute, and the concern for the character of middle-class America—the languages used to discuss these topics interconnect and support each other. Meaning derived in one context informs the understanding of words in another.[2]

Whereas organizations such as Focus shape languages that fuse political, sexual, and theological concerns, academic texts analyzing these debates see the conservative Christian position as motivated primarily by either religion or politics. Therefore, our inquiry requires not only understanding what is religiously at stake for organizations such as Focus but, more fundamentally, providing a new theoretical framework that makes such understanding possible in the first place.

Acknowledging this relationship between political, sexual, and religious concerns in the debates about gays and lesbians demands a fresh analysis of the nature of religious claims in our polity. Like sociologist of religion Robert Wuthnow, I am particularly interested in the transformations that American religion undergoes and their effects on our polity.[3] Yet America is not alone in this process of religious-cum-political change.

Gleaning insights from other places where religion transforms itself and the state will be an important tool for rethinking the systematic issue of how religion and politics interrelate. Therefore, I will examine findings from studies of religious and political revivals in South Asian Buddhism and Hinduism, such as those by Stanley Tambiah and Partha Chatterjee. I will argue that, like the South Asian innovators, conservative Christian leaders promote a religious and political revitalization of America and Christianity. For them a reinvigorated Christianity means new strength for the American nation. The language of this revival is effective because religious themes (such as the power of God) resonate in complex ways with those of sexuality (the power of husbands) and politics (the need to submit to the authority of a Christian nation). Importantly, the South Asian examples demonstrate that such revivals transform what counts as normative religion (Buddhism, Hinduism, or in our case Christianity). Using these insights to carefully analyze American discussions about marriage will then allow us to realize how and why such a transformation of religion in the modern nation-state is inextricably linked to issues of sexuality.

It is important to note at the outset my argument that these American sexual and political theologies forge identities characterized by deep tensions: The Christian man has to embody both aggression and humble submission; the ideal Christian wife is submissive but empowered to resist abusive male aggression. What will appear in my analysis is not a clear set of stable sexual and political identities but a never-ending dance of agency. In it Christians negotiate in their bodies interrelated contradictions between stratifying middle-class respectability and allegedly class-transcending romance, sexual activity and passivity, and divine and human power. The Christian American middle-class body is thus shaped as a field of conflicts. It is the silent incarnation of a message surprisingly similar to what theologian Mark Jordan, in a critique of conservative positions on same-sex marriage, outlines as an ideal marriage theology: "My idealized marriage theology would prevent persons from settling too quickly on any account of their own lives. . . . *It would do this by recalling as often as necessary how difficult it is to tell what divine agency might look like in erotically coupled lives.*"[4] Before entering into the thicket of these arguments, let me address the question of how to delineate the group of conservative Christians whose resistance to same-sex love is at issue.

WHO ARE THE CONSERVATIVE CHRISTIANS, AND WHY THE FOCUS ON
FOCUS ON THE FAMILY?

Far from being a single unified political movement, what we call conservative Christian organizations form a tapestry of groups comprising people with complex sets of ideas and practices. We find innovative city-dwelling Evangelicals who attend urban mega-churches and faithful listeners to programs such as the late Jerry Falwell's *Gospel Hour*.[5] What unites this wide-ranging family of Christians?

One possible answer is the faithful adherence to a set of particular reformed beliefs, such as the inerrancy of the Bible. For example, William Shea characterizes conservative Christians as those practicing "Bible Christianity." This, he states, is the type of Christianity that does not need church or liturgy because it relies on the authority of the Bible alone.[6] This definition may sound like a compelling attempt to trace back the roots of a modern religious phenomenon into the Reformation of the sixteenth century.[7] However, we should remember that American Christians do have churches (mega-churches) and very highly produced liturgies (with Christian pop). Incidentally, sociologist Alan Wolfe makes the exact opposite claim: Contemporary Evangelicals are not at all heirs to the Protestant Reformers. Wolfe explains that they do not faithfully transmit reformed doctrines of sin.[8]

We can quickly see that the project of defining conservative Christianity based on substantive theological doctrines requires some further theological discussions about the precise meaning of these doctrines– and more theology than most sociologists writing on conservative Christians provide. Also, we would need to assume that individual Christians hold beliefs in line with unchangeable doctrines. In short, I am weary of engaging the theological question of who is and who is not a faithful heir to a sixteenth-century movement. And I agree with Greeley and Hout that we should not overlook the differences in context and meaning between Reformation doctrine and the beliefs held by today's conservative Christians. Although certain formulations may seem to use language similar to that of the Reformers, today's religious and political needs shape how ordinary conservative Christians understand their heritage and their beliefs. They engage in conversations about the reach and character of their churches with today's vocabulary. These contemporary conversations help them to revitalize their present communities, dispute within them, and set themselves apart from other Christians or from the "world." Instead of characterizing conservative Christians as those who faithfully adhere to a certain set of precepts, I suggest the following definition: Conservative Christians in America today are those who are being claimed by and are using a certain way of speaking, one whose history is connected to the European and American reformations.[9]

For example, consider the question, "Do you accept Jesus Christ as your personal lord and savior?" This question (and the concern for another person's eternal salvation) will be recognizable for any Southern Baptist, Assembly of God, or Pentecostal Christian—in short, for anyone who considers himself or herself to be emphatically Christian. Roman Catholics share the theological undergrowth of the idea that Jesus wants to have a personal relationship with his faithful. After all, the ideal of the personal savior reaches into a medieval movement, called the *devotio moderna*, that predates the ecclesiological divisions of the Reformation. Yet the question, "Do you accept Jesus Christ as your personal lord and savior?" is alien to a Roman Catholic's vocabulary. In other words, the theological concept may be shared by Christians of different denominations, but the language of having a "personal lord and savior" is not. Thus, although those who speak this language may disagree about what receiving the Lord entails, they can bond over their disagreements because they will recognize each other in using a similar dialect, as it were. Other Christians share other questions and disagreements, such as the belief in the real presence of Christ in the Eucharist, for example. Besides the language of receiving Christ, which for a Catholic would imply partaking in the sacraments, conservative Christians recognize each other by talking about the inerrant truth of the Bible and about the importance of evangelizing the world. Yet, again, the concern about biblical truth is not absent from other denominations. The Roman Catholic Catechism teaches that "we must acknowledge that the books of Scripture firmly, faithfully, and without error teach that truth which God, for the sake of our salvation, wished to see confided to the Sacred Scriptures."[10] The language of the Catechism is easily recognizable for Roman Catholics, and likewise the language of biblical literalism is familiar for conservative Christians. One need not have a precise understanding of the

5

content of the doctrines at stake, but the formulations carry with themselves a deep familiarity. They evoke a tone of voice, a cadence, and immediate associations for those steeped in the specific dialect of his or her church.

These languages may serve as rallying points around which to close ranks and to define in-groups and out-groups. As heirs to the extensive conversations of the Continental and English reformations, conservative Christians will talk and think about the saving encounter with Christ primarily through an idiom involving reading the Bible. Therefore, I understand conservative Christian denominations as characterized by the following use of language: The languages of biblical inerrancy, personal salvation, and evangelism serve as touchstones to define the church in its internal conflicts and those involving others who claim to be Christians. Because African American churches have different political outlooks and socioeconomic backgrounds, as well as different dialects, I follow Greeley and Hout in not considering them as part of the family of conservative Christianity under consideration in this book.[11]

If it is not the historical doctrines of reformed theology but modes of speech that characterize the family of conservative Christians, the following question arises: What shapes these characteristic Christian dialects? And instead of finding the center of gravity for these conversations in the history of reformed theology, I consider contemporary media organizations to be important conduits through which conservative Christians find and hone their dialects. In particular, we will consider in this book the case of James Dobson, the founder of the immensely influential ministry, counseling, and media organization Focus on the Family. His is one of the most influential organizations in shaping conservative Christian culture. The words with which Jack Graham, then president of the Southern Baptist convention, celebrated Focus's twenty-five-year anniversary and James Dobson's contribution to American Christianity are not without merit: "I think a generation has been changed, an entire generation of Christians and families have been changed by the biblical and practical counsel and guidance from Dr. Dobson." This endorsement by the Southern Baptist convention, which is notoriously critical of para-church organizations, shows the profound influence Dobson's organization has in the field of conservative Christianity. Graham lists the achievements as follows: Focus has more than a thousand employees and a budget of more than $125 million, its broadcasts are distributed over a network of thousand radio stations and reach audiences worldwide, and Dobson's film series have had audiences of more than 70 million people.[12] By this reckoning Dobson is one of the most important theologians when it comes to shaping how Americans think about God, the nation, and the family.[13]

Indeed, instead of being a steward of unchanging reformed Bible-based Christianity, Focus is an example of the continuous revitalization of conservative Christianity. As a former professor of child psychology, Dobson founded Focus originally as an advice ministry for parents and became successful with this "Dare to Discipline" approach. These roots place the organization firmly in the religious transformations of the 1960 and 1970s, when after decades of resistance conservative Christianity fully integrated psychological ideas of therapy.[14] Whereas Alan Wolfe sees this turn to self-help language as a rejection of traditional Protestantism, James D. Hunter sees it as an accommodation of modernity that strengthens conservative Christian denominations.[15] Conservative Christian language is born again through the incorporation of therapeutic ideals.

The strength of this innovative strategy can be seen in Focus's success. Its videos, CDs, radio programs, pamphlets, and Web sites reach a great number of consumers across the denominational spectrum and deep into the U.S. political mainstream. Focus's magazine for teen girls, *Brio*, claims to have 180,000 subscribers, and its counterpart for boys, *Breakaway*, has 80,000 subscribers. The *Focus on the Family* magazine reaches more than 2 million readers.[16] These Americans listen to Dobson's message for advice on how to raise their children, create stable families and marriages, and become better Christians. The language used by Focus on the Family resonates well with ordinary conservative Christians, who feel that Focus expresses what they think.[17] Its triple role as media, advice, and ministry organization establishes a feedback loop between the producers and consumers of Focus media, who turn to it with their problems and questions. Each month Focus's staff receives and answers hundreds of thousand letters from its listeners, as Sara Diamond notes.[18] Focus trains pastors, sells courses on DVD about the Christian life, the Bible, and parenting to parishes and individual Christians, and provides churches with study materials for their education programs.

The Internet presence of Focus demonstrates well that this is an organization embedded in and spinning a wide web of references and discourses. More inspirational sites (such as Dobson's Family Guide) are linked to other Web sites presenting allegedly scientific information about homosexuality, and from there we can click to pages about how to make schools safe for Christian children and connect to Citizenlink, Focus's explicitly political information site. Many Focus sites also offer links to coming-out-of-homosexuality groups such as Desert-Stream and Exodus International or other Christian Right groups such as Phyllis Schlafly's Eagle Forum. Its eminent position in this network of mediated discourses makes Focus an excellent site on which to study the languages mobilized for the rejection of same-sex love. Thus, I treat Focus not simply as an isolated example of how conservative Christian organizations speak about same-sex love but also as a main producer and distributor of such speech.[19] As a producer of conservative Christian language, Focus creates hypertexts, that is, texts consisting of words that are linked to many other texts, with varying themes, surroundings, and genres. My analysis of what these texts say about gays and lesbians will demonstrate that the variety of themes and approaches amounts not to a cacophony of voices but to a very tightly controlled message. What is said on Focus's Web sites about gays or lesbians is connected to a very clear set of narrative scripts.[20]

Analyzing these interrelated scripts and understanding their message requires a specific mode of reading. In particular we need a framework that allows us to see as intertwined the different languages Focus uses to talk about sexuality, religion, and politics. These special languages are not independent linguistic systems that connect with one another only tangentially. In other words, religious language is not a subset of political language (or vice versa); neither one is completely disconnected from the other.

CONNECTION TO PREVIOUS RESEARCH

The current scholarship on what motivates Christian resistance to same-sex love is divided between scholars who explain the issue in terms of either political or religious interests. The former camp treats these conservative Christian organizations like any other pressure group, thereby failing to evaluate the religious language that motivates the attitude of many ordinary Christians on questions of homosexuality. The latter camp discusses various religious issues but is perplexed by the fact that these organizations insist that the stability of our polity is at stake when it comes to same-sex marriage.

For example, sociologist of religion Alan Wolfe claims that Americans have differences over "gay marriage, because some of us are conservatives and others are liberals, not because some of us are religious and others secular."[21] Wolfe knows that the probability of finding a person who opposes such marriages is highest among those professing to be conservative Christians. Yet this correlation is not sufficient to establish a causal link from religious to political beliefs. Rather, Wolfe seems to assume that political interests motivate the use of religious language in our debates about so-called cultural issues. Ordinary Americans are alienated by these debates, and ordinary Evangelicals are far more pragmatic in their outlooks than the excited rhetoric of their elites. Consequently, Wolfe characterizes leaders of conservative Christian organizations such as Dobson and Jerry Falwell as media figures and political players.[22] They are minions for the efforts to mobilize a Republican base of voters for economic policies that cannot otherwise find a majority. Wolfe's argument requires us to believe that organizations such as Focus on the Family (and the numerous churches in which pastors preach against the "sin" of homosexuality) do not pursue religious interests but are akin to political pressure groups. And we must assume that voters who reject marriage for gays and lesbians are not motivated by the prevalent rhetoric that many church organizations circulate into the wider American public. Likewise, Edward Glaeser and Bryce Ward, who studied the connection between religious and voting preferences in U.S. politics, suggest that churches or other such organizations can serve as a network to send political messages to mobilize a voter base. Although they caution against equating religious with political values, they see the difference between two in the fact that religious views are held more fervently than positions on other topics. They conclude that this disparity in emotional attachment makes religious views useful mobilization tools for politicians.[23]

The problem with Wolfe's and Glaeser and Ward's model is that religious values appear only as handmaidens for ulterior political interests, useful for their mobilizing force but not formative for true political concerns. We will discuss Wolfe's arguments in detail in chapter 2, especially his claim that conservative Christians in the United States are religious innovators and not conserving inheritors of traditional Protestant values. His arguments allow us to analyze the importance of Christian media organizations such as Focus for the formation of religious interests in our polity. However, if we want to take seriously what ordinary conservative Christians think about sexual policies in the United States, then we should not overlook that they use religious language to express their beliefs.

Whereas political concerns are decisive for Wolfe, others think primarily theological questions are at stake in the debates about gays and lesbians. Before we turn to these literatures let me flag one point: Glaeser, Ward, Wolfe, and most of the theologians who debate the issue share the problematic preconception that religious and political beliefs belong to different systemic spheres. Here are the religious beliefs that are formed independently of politics and that can be used (or neglected) by politicians, and here are political concerns that are shaped without connection to religious values or institutions. Broadening our horizons beyond the U.S. context by incorporating in the next chapter scholarship from other geographic areas, such as South Asia, will help us to overcome this misconception. For now, let us turn to works in the study of religion that see the debate about gay and lesbian sex as motivated primarily by religious concerns.

Many contemporary Christian theologians evaluate erotic love between people of the same sex from the perspective of religious ethics, scripture, ecclesiology, or systematic reflections on the nature of God. From these literatures, we can learn how Christian thinkers wrestle with the issue in multifaceted and complex ways. Here is not the place to present these debates. Let me mention only that based on a deep analysis of the multiple doctrinal issues involved, some theologians, such as Eugene Rogers, argue that marriage-like gay or lesbian relationships are theologically productive and justified. He argues that embracing them is not a matter of giving in to so-called liberal political demands but one of deepening our understanding of the divine. In fact, far from finding a unified theological position if we survey Christian theology on the issue, we see that the debate about gay and lesbian sexuality extends into the most central Christian doctrines, such as the belief in the incarnation or resurrection. They raise the issue of what role our sexual bodies are supposed to play in the drama of salvation.[24]

Given this diversity of theological opinion, we should be wary of the claim that a certain position on sexuality represents *the* teaching of true Christianity. In *Blessing Same-Sex Unions* Mark Jordan argues this point historically by showing that instead of a unified Christian marriage tradition we find lineages of contestations and disputes. These theological literatures can remind us of the fact that religious traditions such as Christianity are complex entities with convoluted histories.

However, it is problematic that these scholars seem to place Christian religious beliefs in a political vacuum. They assume that the claims of German theologian Karl Barth, who lived during the terrors of Nazi Germany, for example, can be weighted against those of a monk from medieval Italy, Thomas Aquinas. The character and content of religious beliefs (and of the act of believing religiously) seem unaffected by whether we live in a modern nation-state during the apocalypse of German fascism or in a feudal empire. Jordan's work, which we will discuss in more detail in chapter 3, is the notable exception. He shows how modern ideas of romance, which are kept in circulation by a veritable marriage industry, are deeply implicated in how contemporary Americans speak and think about human sexuality or about the revelation of God's love. Jordan is pained by the fact that America's religious language is infiltrated by the romantic chatter from magazines, Hollywood movies, romance novels, and the like. It is noteworthy that in contrast to the other theologians writing on gays or lesbians and their love, Jordan sees how extra-theological forces shape profoundly how and what Americans believe about the religious value of erotic love.[25]

In contrast to the abstractions of academic theology, works in the sociology of religion aim to find out the lived theologies of ordinary Christians. Here we find two approaches: interpretations of general surveys such as Christian Smith's *Christian America: What Evangelicals Really Want* and Andrew Greeley and Michael Hout's *The Truth About Conservative Christians* or ethnographic studies such as Sally Gallagher's *Evangelical Identity and Gendered Family Life*, Marie Griffith's *God's Daughters: Evangelical Women and Power of Submission*, or Dawn Moon's *God, Sex, and Politics: Homosexuality and Everyday Theologies.*[26]

Smith was one of the first to combat the stereotype of conservative Christians as the extremist foot soldiers in America's "culture wars," who were being duped into action by minority economic interests.[27] Smith's and Greeley and Hout's interpretations of numerous survey data draw a complex picture of how ordinary American Christians negotiate the demands of changing economic and cultural circumstances. Instead of a mass of ideologues repeating uniform ideas of theology, gender, and the nation, we see in these studies pragmatic Americans holding complex and at times contradictory opinions.[28] This awareness of the complexities in the lives of ordinary conservative Christians has led to a reorientation of scholarship away from works on the Evangelical elite to focused and detailed studies of the lives of ordinary Christians.

Although the shift to the local has an impressive pedigree in religious studies, I argue that it is important to account for the translocal quality of religious language as well.[29] This means that paying attention to elite media organizations is required if we want to understand how conservative Christians talk about same-sex love in a specific way. Let me clarify briefly the centrality of Christian media in shaping conservative religious and political beliefs by explaining why we need to look at a level between general surveys and ethnographic studies of specific church communities.

In their *Love the Sin: Sexual Regulation and the Limits of Religious Tolerance*, Janet Jakobsen and Anne Pellegrini describe the central role that specifically conservative Christianity plays in the shaping of moral debates in America. Not Christianity as such but a specific form of conservative Christian Protestantism exerts its power over how Americans understand normative sexuality, they argue. A quick glance at surveys of the Pew Foundation supports this point.[30] Here we learn that opposition to allowing same-sex couples to marry varies by Christian denomination. For the year 2006 the numbers are as follows: "White evangelical Protestants (78%) and black Protestants (74%) overwhelmingly oppose gay marriage, as do a majority of white Catholics (58%) and a plurality of white mainline Protestants (47%). Only among seculars does a majority (63%) express support for gay marriage." Compare this with the following findings from the Gallup Foundation about the percentages of religious respondents *in favor* of marriage for gays and lesbians in Europe. For the fifteen states of old Europe (i.e., before a number of Eastern European states were admitted in 2004) the numbers were as follows: "Christians (53%) and Muslims (54%) tend to be slightly less favourable [toward marriage rights for gays and lesbians] than other religious groups (59%)."[31] Thus, Muslims in old Europe favored marriage rights for gays and lesbians on the same level as mainline Protestants in the United States. These statistical findings show that not Christianity as an abstract entity but specific denominational attitudes and beliefs that are related to specific political and cultural locales correlate with a person's opposition to such marriages.

What are the attitudes and beliefs that motivate American conservative Christians to reject the idea of marriage for gays and lesbians? The stock answer is that the belief that the Bible is literally true explains why American conservative Christians think differently from other Christians about gays and lesbians. Indeed, the notion that belief in biblical inerrancy is the key factor in Evangelical attitudes toward sexuality is a staple in the scholarship on conservative Christians, as anthropologist Sally Gallagher points out.[32] Yet Gallagher cautions us not to embraces this scholarly consensus too quickly. Perhaps surprisingly, her studies do not confirm the thesis that belief in biblical literalism is the main reason why Evangelical Christians embrace a discourse that upholds so-called traditional gender roles.[33] To my mind, the point of this critique is not to dismiss the answers that such Christians give in surveys and interviews but to acknowledge that conservative Christian attitudes toward their scriptures are complex. If a Christian says, "I believe this because the Bible tells me so," the matter might be closed for her; after all, she knows what it means to believe something on the authority of scripture (and the Holy Spirit). But do we—as scholars and fellow citizens—know what this means? We will learn in the next chapter more about the theological ideals implied in reading the Bible and discerning its unfailing truth.

Although reference to an abstract doctrine of the inerrancy of the Bible does not help us understand what motivates conservative Christians in their rejection of erotic love of gays and lesbians, another correlation does. Gallagher finds that the hours spent consuming conservative Christian media can serve as an indicator for how deeply a person is embedded in conservative Christian culture. Consumption of these media products does not *cause* Christians to think about gay or lesbian sex in a certain manner. Yet studying the language that circulates between consumers and producers of

13

Christian media brings to the fore the themes, images, and concerns associated with gay and lesbian Americans. I am particularly interested in tracing the connections between religious, sexual, and political narratives in how conservative Christian organizations present and evaluate erotic love of gays and lesbians.

The importance of media organizations in the landscape of contemporary religious life is not surprising. It is well documented in other cases, such as in what Olivier Roy calls the Islamic revival.[34] Some would say that it is a hallmark of the transformation of contemporary religion that its practices and symbols cease to be unquestionably embedded in circumscribed local communities.[35] Because they are disconnected from the stabilities of traditional local milieus, the meaning of these practices and symbols needs constant attention (and is a source of ongoing worries). We find texts with titles such as *What Is Islam?* and *The Christian Dad's Answer Book*, aimed not at so-called outsiders but at practitioners of the religion in question. Like the first catechisms, which originated in the European wars of religion, these texts make their religions into objects in need of definition.[36] The need for such definitions apparently did not arise for those living in a monoculture where work, communal festivals, and the exchanges of goods and stories were interspersed with the rhythm of a largely unified religious practice. However, as Alan Wolfe's work shows, ordinary conservative Christians do not live in such cultural isolation. They are among the most itinerant and seeking groups in America.[37]

In these situations of mobility, where the boundaries of a religious identity are fluid, institutions that span different localities and unite them into a virtual community become important. Currently, this is particularly true of groups with a strong radio, TV, and (with increasing impact) Internet presence. In the case of Islam, Oliver Roy shows how a network of media organizations shapes a common religious language for populations with diverse geographic and cultural origins.[38] I will argue that something similar is true for mobile middle-class Americans who are conservative Christians. Conservative Christian media, counseling, and ministry groups offer (with input from different localities) translocal religious languages, which constrain and enable the theologizing of ordinary Christians.

These perhaps more theoretical considerations are supported by the fact that ordinary Christians themselves evidently have a vested interest in repeating the language of their elites. For example, Smith's work on the issue of submission shows that ordinary Evangelicals do indeed maintain the language put in circulation by their well-known and vocal institutions. Even if they embrace ideas of gender mutuality and live in complex marital relationships, the Evangelicals studied by Smith still engage in and maintain the language of male headship.[39] And the ethnographies of Griffith and Harding can explain why this linguistic continuity is so important. They point out that conservative Christians want to join "a narrative tradition," to use a phrase coined by Harding.[40] That is, through the acts of telling and listening to stories about male headship and female submission, the dangers of same-sex love, and the promises of heterosexual intercourse, these Christians embrace a way of being in the world. Harding argues that by circulating these narratives, Christians find and order what they know about themselves and the world in which they live. The narrative traditions (embedded in prayers, radio conversations, and other forms of communication) that their media and ministry organizations circulate allow these Christians to express themselves.

At the same time, this language functions to *shape* the experience of individual Christians, aiming to reorganize how the born-again Christian sees herself and the world.[41] According to Harding, conversion involves taking on the linguistic scripts offered by the Evangelical communities. For example, in Griffith's and Harding's empathetic studies we see how individual Christian women negotiate the narrative scripts about sexuality, faith, and the family that circulate in their communities. Yet we also see that these ordinary Evangelical women hold onto these languages and realign their experiences with them. In sum, analyzing the language produced and disseminated by the religious elites can give us insights into how ordinary conservative Christians conceive of sexuality, politics, and religion.

Importantly, this language resonates with a wider American public. Consider the following peculiarity. In 2003, Pew researchers asked respondents who objected to legalizing marriage for gay and lesbian couples for their reasons. When asked in an open format, the objectors produced a whole variety of issues. Only 17 percent answered, "It is against my religious beliefs"; another 28 percent gave answers that the Pew Foundation grouped together under "It is morally wrong/sinful/the Bible says so." This is a total of 45 percent who named some form of religious reason (if moral reasons are equated with religious ones, as Pew evidently did). The picture changed when the researchers asked in a closed format why the interviewees rejected allowing such marriages. Eighty-two percent of the opponents of "gay marriage" agreed with the statement, "Gay marriage goes against my religious beliefs." The difference is even more dramatic for the statement "Gay marriage undermines the traditional family," which appears over and over again in conservative Christian literatures on the issue. In the open format, only 1 percent of interviewees who rejected legalizing same-sex marriage gave this argument as a reason for their position, yet 56 percent of all Americans, and 76 percent of those who reject marriage for gay couples, agreed with the statement if presented with it in a closed format. Americans have differing rationales for their position, depending on whether they express their opposition in their own words or use language brought into public circulation by conservative Christian organizations.[42]

The narratives shaped by media and ministry groups such as Focus apparently help many respondents, who otherwise may not be able find the right words for their sentiments, to express their uneasiness with love between men or between women. (As some political theorists claim, these Christian organizations can be seen as providing shortcuts for Americans to make up their minds on an issue of public morality. Instead of engaging in prolonged discussions, they can tap into the narrative scripts provided by Focus on the Family and invest more time in economic pursuits.)[43] Therefore, I agree with sociologist of religion James D. Hunter, who argues that "the options [with which ordinary Americans ended up] were framed by elites in the parties and special interest organizations, their respective institutions, and the rank-and-file supporters who formed the grassroots support. So, too, were the narratives that contextualized and the arguments that legitimated those choices."[44]

In sum, I suggest that we turn to studying the language produced by conservative Christian elites, specifically the languages they use to talk publicly about love between Americans of the same sex. To this end I will weave together a number of literatures (theology, sociology or anthropology of religion, and gender studies). Although I am skeptical about some of the theoretical assumptions of sociologists such as Wolfe, I will refer to their data if doing so furthers our understanding of the texts this book analyzes. In particular, however, I will relate back our analysis of discourses circulated through media to the findings of qualitative anthropologies, such as the works of Gallagher, Griffith, and Moon. I consider their works to be representative for the most fine-grained analyses of religious language among conservative Christians. This conversation with local anthropological studies will help to establish how the narrative traditions we examine appear through local and translocal circulations of words and ideas.

After a brief overview of the arguments of this book in the next section, I will explain in more detail the theoretical and methodological underpinnings of my analysis. Doing so at the end of this chapter will allow readers who are not immediately interested in such theoretical and methodological contextualization to delve into the body of this study after the following short chapter outline. Let me mention only shortly one point pertaining to the larger architecture of this study: It focuses on language circulated through Focus on the Family. Yet before we can analyze Focus's texts in detail (as in chapters 4 and 5) we must establish two things: First, in chapter 2 I develop a reading strategy that allows my readers to see as interrelated the different languages Focus uses to talk about sexuality, religion, and politics. I do this by engaging current scholarship on conservative Christian organizations, including work on Focus, and by discussing the complex attitudes toward the Bible prevalent in texts produced by such organizations, including Focus itself. Second, chapter 3 shows how Focus's ideas about Christian heterosexual marriage are intertwined with those shared by a broader middle-class American mainstream. Both chapters (2 and 3) introduce the topic of activity and passivity as a leitmotif for my analysis of the religious, sexual, and political texts of Focus in the remaining chapters. In general my interpretation is guided by the intent to show Focus not as an isolated organization but as one that has extended its reach into multiple locales and one that is profoundly connected with other producers of conservative Christian culture.

17

STRUCTURE OF THE BOOK

In chapter 2 I argue that conservative Christian narratives about same-sex couples and their love are motivated neither by a doctrinal belief in biblical literalism nor by exclusively political concerns. Rather, I demonstrate how

cultural and hence political contexts shape the reading of the biblical text
and how it appears to be true for Christians. To see more clearly this intertwining of religious and political language, I turn to scholarship outside the
American context. Reviewing some examples from Hinduism and South
Asian Buddhism I argue that religious revival movements evoke the idea of
a timeless tradition in order to reject the authority of previous elites and to
endorse new religious and political regimes. Religious convictions in these
cases are both public and political. They are produced in a political process, and they shape it. Therefore analyzing the fine points of biblical texts
without reference to the context of their political use or treating conservative Christian groups as yet another type of political pressure group is not
helpful for understanding what is at stake for conservative Christians.
Rather, we have to examine the confluence of political and religious forces
in America that shape both political and religious convictions about appropriate forms of sexual behavior in state and family.

This is the goal of chapter 3, where, given the history of the institution
of marriage in America, I analyze what conservative Christian organizations say about allowing marriage for same-sex couples. Here I will show
how religious concerns are part of the shaping of American national identity and how central the institution of marriage is for this process, via the
ideals of romantic love and respectable middle-class sexuality. What counts
as acceptable and as traditional Christian marriage theology develops in
the context of political interests that form and support the modern nation-
state. At the same time, these interests are shaped through language and
images related to Christianity. Religious and political languages are co-
produced and reinforce each other.

Chapter 4 examines how Focus on the Family imagines same-sex love
and its threat to the heterosexual order. We will see that male—rather than
female—homosexuals are talked about most often in Focus literature.
Within it, two specific stereotypical images of gays are depicted, which I
call the oversexed hyper-male and a gender-insecure hypo-male. I argue that
these two images delineate normative Christian masculinity as an unstable
composite of dominant aggression and submission. The masculinized lesbian, or the feminist, on the other hand, operates in tandem with these
depictions of male homosexuality. Particularly in discourses of proper female

submission to male headship, Focus's texts invoke the dangerous influence of feminism as confusing women about the value of Christian submission. Feminists and lesbians are portrayed as women who reject the right male authority over their lives. Yet what submission is remains unclear both in Focus's texts and in the lives of many ordinary Evangelicals. Instead of an unambiguous picture of Christian masculinity or femininity, the texts of Focus present us with a normative Christian sexuality that is fraught with tensions and ambiguity. The rhetorical construction of gays, lesbians, and feminists helps to outline the shapes of normative masculinity and femininity; evoking the images of these transgressing sexualities is part of a strategy enabling a field of contestation for what it means to be a Christian man or woman.

In the final chapter I argue that conservative Christian language about same-sex love connects with and reinforces the shaping of middle-class sexualities as mechanisms for the hierarchical distribution of power. Such power is thus political, sexual, and theological. The narrative inventions of the feminist lesbian, the gender-disturbed gay or his oversexed counterpart, and the painful image of the abused wife function like an arena: They present the space for a deep play where spectators and actors alike can get lost in performing with overdrawn clarity the tensions of the American sexual regime. Here it is clear what makes men into men, and women into women, yet here too is the place where the impossibilities of American and Christian sexualities are lived out.

Before I end this introduction with some more theoretical reflections on the character of this book, let me mention one terminological issue. I use rather fluidly the terms *sex*, *sexuality*, and *gender*. For those who have thought hard about the relationship between biological sex and cultural gender markers, this may be disappointing. And I clearly do not want to imply that sex equals gender in a deterministic sense, as if how we present or experience ourselves as men or women is determined by biology or sex hormones (see chapter 4). Yet deciding whether something constitutes sexual behavior or gender behavior is difficult. The expectations about what constitutes acceptable cultural gender roles shape how sexuality is experienced and lived out—and, conversely, expectations of and fears about where and how we find sexual gratification control gender ideals. This point is driven home by the fact that the resistance against legitimizing the love of two men or two women seems rooted not only in assumptions about cultural gender but also in what we do with our sex organs.

Consider the case of the recently publicized "overview" of medical literature concerned with the alleged pathophysiology of male homosexuality by Dr. James Holsinger (once a Republican nominee for the office of surgeon general). In 1991 he put this document together for a workshop in which members of his Methodist church discussed the topic of homosexuality. The alleged harm done to the male anus in homosexual intercourse is the key concern of the text. Holsinger acknowledges that heterosexual women engage in anal intercourse as well and that they do so without incurring physical or mental trauma. Why is homosexual male anal intercourse medically problematic? Holsinger finds the answer for this question in a medical study of this sexual practice and writes, "Forceful anal penetration without lubrication against a resistant sphincter will result in abrasive . . . and psychic trauma."[45]

Holsinger's underlying assumption is apparently that men anally penetrate other men mostly without lubrication, against resistance, and violently. This is clearly a hypothesis grounded in ideas about normative male sexuality. A man could never enjoy being anally penetrated, and therefore he needs to resist, or a man would never perform this act with another man using as much gentleness and care as he would if a woman were involved. Conversely, it seems as if women are not prone to resistance. Cultural assumptions about male and female sexuality—about what they enjoy in their bodies and how they normatively act—inform how Christians such as Dr. Holsinger read the scientific literature about alleged sexual pathologies. Fears and assumptions surrounding the sex act (where and how one finds sexual gratification and what we do with our sexual organs) are at issue. Given such interconnections between ideas about sexuality and gender, I think that a clear sex–gender distinction is misleading in our context. Therefore I will use the terms interchangeably. The context will show where I want to emphasize an issue of cultural ideas about sexuality, an issue of sexual love, or one of reproductive biology.

20

THEORETICAL CONSIDERATIONS AND
METHODOLOGICAL CONSEQUENCES

What is the theoretical context of my analysis, and how does this context affect my methodological decisions about which materials to examine, how to use previous anthropological research, and how to position my own interpretive effort?

THEORETICAL PRESUPPOSITION: BELIEFS ARE PUBLIC

At its core, this book is an exercise in understanding the shared language that conservative Christians use when talking about same-sex love.[46] I treat this language as a social fact, that is, as a reality that is open for public investigation. By talking about language as social fact, I want to highlight that I am interested in beliefs as they are formed in publicly shared propositions. Holding such a belief is a public practice, even if the belief in question involves a matter of our private conscience such as religion or attitudes about sexuality. After all, language is necessary to form beliefs (even those that we voice only to ourselves), and speaking involves a shared community.

The philosophical background of my focus is Ludwig Wittgenstein's rejection of the idea of a private language. Although the reader of this book should not expect a treatise about the finer points of a contested philosophical issue, let me mention some core elements as they relate to our investigation. (Those interested in a fuller and more technical discussion of this argument can turn to the relevant chapters of my book *Beyond the Philosopher's Fear*.)[47] We can understand the heart of Wittgenstein's insight by asking, "What would be the opposite of things that we hold to be true by using shared language?" For a Wittgensteinian, the contrasting idea is not "things we hold to be true by using a private language that is available only to an individual herself." Rather, the relevant contrast is "other things that we hold to be true by using publicly shared language."

Thus, by focusing on propositions as they are formed in public language, I do not want to invite the claim that people say one thing in public but think another in the privacy of their skulls, as it were. Such a claim would presuppose the very idea that Wittgenstein rejects, namely that we could conceive of beliefs beyond the reach of language. This presupposition does not make sense: Imagine someone asks you, "How do you feel? Any different from yesterday?" You can perhaps point to vague and fleeting prelinguistic attitudes, feelings, and so on, but when you want to describe what they are or to identify whether the feeling you have today is similar to the one you had yesterday, you need to turn to language.[48]

Conceiving of beliefs as social facts does not commit me to the position that their meanings are controlled by social forces that are imagined to be beyond an individual's input. In the philosophical debates about Wittgenstein's vision of language, the character of the social forces that shape what we can say and mean is discussed, perhaps somewhat idiosyncratically, under the rubric of grammar. Whereas *grammar* for many linguists refers to syntactic rules governing the formation of correct nouns, verbs, and so on, Wittgenstein is interested in the semantic rules governing the correct meaning of words. For Wittgenstein these limits on how to successfully use words are established in our acts of speaking together. Grammar therefore is not a system of rules that is given by the structures of language itself or found as hard wired into the brains of language users. In this sense grammar does not determine each individual speech act. Rather, grammar emerges out of our acts of speaking together. The web of shared speech precedes each individual utterance and thus establishes a field of expectations about what constitutes correct, outrageous, innovative, or sly speech (to name just a few possibilities of evaluating language). Yet each speech act itself feeds into and thus modifies the network of shared language. Free jazz improvisation, rather than classical variation on a theme, may be the most apt representation of Wittgenstein's vision of what establishes normativity in language. We cannot predict on the basis of the constraints of a genre or the rules of modulation what counts as an appropriate move (in tonality, timbre, or key). Rather, appropriateness (or inappropriateness) reveals itself in the act of improvising and in the audience's reaction. Whether a move fails or succeeds cannot be determined from what came before. The listeners' willingness to follow and to accept an unexpected move, to appreciate the outrageous as novel, will establish what can count as "in line" with the normative use of musical moves (or words). Accordingly, both the improvisations and their receptions establish the outlines of what constitutes grammatical correctness.[49]

In this sense, I want to distance myself somewhat from some theories that see an ideological force as operating covertly in language, a force that is said to determine meaning without input or knowledge of individual speakers. In contrast, I think that the struggles for linguistic control through media, professional organizations, parents, communal leaders (including cool peers and wise elders), and the like are overtly on display. Indeed, waged in middle-school cafeterias and political war rooms, these struggles rely on the insight or intuition that language is a tool of social inclusion and exclusion. For example, that language is a means of exercising social power will not come as a surprise to people who as children were punished by their parents or by teachers if they used their home dialect and did not speak "standard" English. Thus I do not consider language use as an ideological practice, which hides its implication in the establishing of hierarchies of power. Nor do I think that language users misrecognize the fact that speaking involves social sorting.[50] Rather, some awareness of the linguistic side of social power is part of having language competence; it is part of the very improvisations that make words go around.

In other words, political interests do not simply use language (Christian or otherwise), but they emerge out of it. Conversely, language use (Christian or otherwise) cannot be separated into apolitical informative and political performative parts. Rather, the grammar of Christian language emerges out of social, and thus politically inflected, practices. Consequently, it would be problematic to search first for the Christian meaning of a particular speech act and then examine its political use or consequences. An analysis of how such speech shapes and negotiates fields of social power is integral to any project that aims to understand Christian language about sexuality.

METHODOLOGICAL CONSEQUENCES

This focus on beliefs as they are formed in shared language has methodological consequences first for my decision to make so-called elite or media discourse the centerpiece of my examination, second for how I treat qualitative anthropological studies, and third for how I conceive of my own interpretive position.

Given that the focus of my study is an understanding of conservative Christian language as social fact, I am not interested in an individual informant's interiority. This means I do not engage in detailed interviews with individual informants of particular locales, as if these Christians possessed a truth that was accessible only to them and that I needed to make public. Rather, I want to understand how, through the sharing of public languages about same-sex love, conservative Christians create, nuance, and maintain particular webs of meanings. I want to listen in, as it were, on their improvisations on the topic of homosexuality by analyzing the narratives, images, and exhortations that circulate in conservative Christian talk about same-sex love.

It is important to note that not all speakers are equal in their ability to circulate language. This inequality is exacerbated by the fact that in highly socially mobile contexts face-to-face interactions and localized church authorities have less and less power to shape the grammar of what can be said in a given religious language. Rather, such grammar is produced through the influences of mass media communications, via radio, video, or the Internet, for example. Para-church and lobbying institutions such as Focus on the Family have a powerful position to echo, amplify, and shape the narrative scripts that conservative Christians share. Conversely, I treat testimonies of individual Christians not as the authentic point of origin of such language but as other relay points, in turn creating, echoing, changing, and further distributing religious language. In examining the findings of selected anthropological works (particularly the studies of Bartkowski, Gallagher, and Griffith), I aim to show how Christians in various locales speak in the idiom familiarized by the various media. Moreover, these works are of particular importance for me because they constitute the beginning of a scholarly examination of the body theologies operative among Evangelical Christians.

What interests me is an understanding of the modes of meaning that are produced in this public network of language circulation between elite and local relay points. What will come to the fore in my analysis is that the linguistic network archives great message control (in the sense that certain tropes of speaking of same-sex love are repeated over and over again, and thus other modes of speaking about such love are crowded out); however, this tightly controlled set of messages about Christian sexuality produces conflict-laden and oscillating body theologies. The ideals of Christian masculinity and femininity emerging in these language circulations are theologically productive precisely because they turn the Christian body into a field of a permanent struggle to find the right balances of sexual, theological, and political power. When does female submission (understood as an active submitting) threaten to turn into the passive enduring of domestic abuse? When does Christian male assertiveness devolve into a pagan arrogance vis-à-vis the divine order, demanding restraint and submission to a higher law? Although I will analyzes these entanglements further, let me mention here that, far from creating simple or premodern scripts for how to be a Christian, the conservative Christian languages about same-sex love shape a complex subjectivity.

In short, I consider this book to be an examination of the "grammar" of the idea of same-sex love in the language circulated by conservative Christian organizations. In particular, my grammatical analysis in this Wittgensteinian sense leads to an inquiry into how the statements conservative Christians make in language and the words they use hang together and form a totality of ideas, attitudes, and judgments.[51] Giving a perspicuous representation of how different parts of our language (concepts and practices) interconnect and interact helps clarify what we mean and can say. As Wittgenstein writes, a "perspicuous representation produces just that [kind of] understanding which consists in 'seeing connections'" between the different instances of a concept.[52] It is important for Wittgenstein that the different examples of a given concept, such as that related to the word *game*, are unified not by a single essence or a single characteristic.[53] Rather, our actions, that is, the practices of using words, of playing, and of representing, hold all these instances of *game* together. Our grammatical investigation therefore can provide a sense for the multifaceted nature and the coherence of various Christian languages about same-sex love. For example, we see teen advice Web sites and parenting manuals evoke language that is repeated in materials for the education of conservative Christian voters, which in turn echoes formulations and arguments about the role of sexuality on marriage counseling sites that are informed by academic anthropologists and psychiatrists. By tracing these connections between political, self-help-oriented, and inspirational languages, for example, we will see how certain ideas about the perils and problems of same-sex love resonate over various registers of language. Indeed, through these intertextual or interdiscursive resonances, conservative Christian language about same-sex love draws into play complex webs of meaning inside and outside strictly Christian language communities.

How do I account for my position in analyzing these resonances? I consider my project of understanding to be both a diagnostic and an interpretive exercise. It is diagnostic by requiring an artificial stop in the ongoing improvisations of language. I am not immediately engaged in the conservative circulations of language about homosexuality. I aim to look at previously played moves to gain a sense of the meanings these languages can enable for those engaged in their circulations. Yet my analysis is also interpretive, because I am asking the texts to provide further religious meanings that are implied in the acts of asserting, for example, that sexual essences are clearly discernible. In so doing, I take seriously the fact that Focus's texts constantly worry about how best to delineate sexual identities on issues such as sexual agency, passivity, and abuse. Thus I follow concerns that are presented in the realm of this discourse itself, as in letters or Q&A sites, which address the question of what constitutes the right level of female submission or of male aggression.

In this diagnostic and interpretive sense, my examination is similar to what discourse theorist Sigfried Jäger says about our ability to critically analyze dominant discourses.[54] Those whose plausibilities are formed under a given set of dominant discourses can nevertheless evaluate and problematize them by tracing how they transport conflicting ideals and represent discourse-immanent tensions. Although this analysis requires a diagnostic stopping of the flow of speech, it does not require a position outside the plausibilities of a given discourse. For example, every Christian theologian can recognize the tensions between human and divine agency in the drama of salvation or the contradictory desire to maintain God's goodness and omnipotence in the face of catastrophic suffering. Not every Christian is a theologian in the sense that he or she stops to reflect on the flow of shared language; yet being a theologian does not entail stopping to be a Christian. In fact, these tensions and contradictions are often considered to be theologically productive by introducing a deeper play of devotion and a more profound sense of divine mystery. Be that as it may, I mention this possibility to trace tensions and contractions from within theological discourse to stress that my interpretive stance neither requires nor precludes a specific religious commitment.

Our quest for a perspicuous representation can be useful in two situations: when we want to understand another person who comes from another culture or when we ourselves are at a loss for words because our own words don't quite seem to reach what we want to say.

As for the first case, in his *Lectures on Religion*, Wittgenstein states that before judging or contradicting a person's religious statement, we need to understand what she means by it. This is not a matter of knowing the dictionary meaning of a word. We have to know which connections she makes between statements or what kind of associations seem natural to her. Wittgenstein himself models how to understand another person who may share the same language but whose words are far removed from what he considers to be meaningful. His waffling over whether to indict a certain Roman Catholic priest of faulty reasoning is an example of Wittgenstein's resistance to using slogans in disputes involving religion. He does not present a theory claiming that religious statements are like code, impossible to understand for the outsider, as some interpretations of Wittgenstein have it. Rather, he shows the hard work involved in understanding one another.[55] Do not pretend too quickly to understand her, and don't give up too quickly on her, either. Try to figure out how this statement makes sense for someone and figure out the contexts and surrounding assumptions that stabilize it.

Understanding a statement such as "homosexuality is sinful" presupposes seeing how it is embedded in other contexts of speech and practice. After all, Wittgenstein thinks that our beliefs form a system in which "some things stand unshakably fast and others are more or less likely to shift. What stands fast, does so not because it is intrinsically obvious or convincing; it is rather held fast by what lies around it."[56] In sum, a Wittgensteinian analysis of grammar probes into the web of plausibilities from which a religious statement draws its strength to convince and to shape decisions and attitudes.

Such analysis is helpful not only for cases in which we are faced with another person whose sentiments, sense of plausibilities, and ideas we do not share. A perspicuous representation can also help when we do not know what to think about something, not because we lack proper information or access to facts but because we don't know what *are* the relevant facts or what would count as factual. We have already seen how many Americans are unclear about why they reject the idea of marriage for couples of the same sex. They somehow feel that such marriages are objectionable, but they do not quite know how to express their reasons. Apparently, many are drawn in conflicting directions, and yet they are influenced by the narratives provided to them by conservative Christian organizations.[57] A grammatical investigation is necessary in precisely these cases, where we are unsure about how to frame an issue or where the concepts we use fail to provide a clear grasp of it.

RELIGIOUS INTERESTS
BETWEEN BIBLE AND POLITICS

I want to begin our project of understanding what conservative Christians say about same-sex love by asking what motivates this discourse. This seems to be an easy question. Is it not apparent that conservative Christians base their beliefs on a literal reading of the Bible? And if it is not the Bible that motivates them, then it must be that conservative politics (and not deep-seated religious convictions) determine how conservative Christians think about same-sex love.

Indeed, the notion that belief in biblical inerrancy is the key factor in their attitudes toward sexuality is a staple in the scholarship about conservative Christians, as anthropologist Sally Gallagher points out.[1] Yet Gallagher also cautions us not to embrace this scholarly consensus too quickly. Conservative Christian attitudes toward their scriptures are rather complex. If a Christian says, "I believe this because the Bible tells me so," the matter might be closed for her; after all, she knows what it means to believe something on the authority of scripture (and the Holy Spirit).

But do we as scholars and fellow citizens know what this means? Rather than taking "because the Bible says so" as an answer, I want to take it as the opening for an inquiry about the role of scripture in forming beliefs about sexuality.

In the first part of this chapter I argue that not abstract belief in biblical inerrancy but the degree to which a person is embedded in a conservative Christian culture influences how she reads scripture. This claim is backed up by Gallagher's statistical evidence, and it also links up with one version of conservative Christian theology of interpreting scripture, as I will show. We can glean this theology by examining how the biblical text is actually read. Conservative Christians discern which interpretation of a biblical passage resonates with them as being truly inspired by the Holy Spirit. These resonances are inevitably influenced by their cultural and political contexts.

Does this mean that political and not religious considerations motivate conservative Christians in rejecting the love between partners of the same sex? In the second section of this chapter I address the argument that political and not religious issues are at stake. We have seen that sociologist of religion Alan Wolfe claims that Americans differ in their attitude toward gay marriage primarily because of their political ideals.[2] It is true that being religious *tout court* is not the issue (even though secular people in both America and Europe are widely in support of the legalization of marriage between people of the same sex). Yet how a person practices her beliefs and to what specific branch of Christianity she belongs seem to predict whether she rejects such marriages.

However, for reasons that will become clearer in this chapter, I find it problematic to distinguish clearly between political and religious motivations in these discussions of sexuality. Instead, I argue that political and religious stories about traditional marriage and "old-time religion" work together in shaping conservative Christian positions on the marriage rights of gays and lesbians. Clarifying this point will require a certain amount of methodological labor. Thus, the second part of this chapter will invest in some more principled reflections on how to think about the intertwining of discourses about politics, sexuality, and religion. To this end I will turn to scholars of South Asian religions who analyzed the relationships between religious and political revivals during the emergence of Sri Lankan or Indian nationalism. Learning from the insights of South Asianists about political Buddhism or Hinduism may seem odd in a book about conservative Christian organizations in America, yet as I will argue, religious actors form their ideas about what Buddhism (or Hinduism or Christianity) should be in relation to political and economic interests. At the same time, such religious values, textual traditions, and practices are part of the processes that organize our polities. Therefore, we cannot evaluate the various religious claims in the debates about same-sex love without first having a better sense about the synergies between modern religion and the modern nation-state. This chapter provides the methodological basis for such an examination, one that continues in chapter 3, which deals with the history and ideal of the Christian and American marriage. Engaging in this kind of foundational discussion will allow us to see the current conflicts about same-sex love as an opportunity to rethink our understanding of the relationship between politics and religion in the modern nation. First, however, let us turn to the claim that a doctrinal belief in biblical inerrancy motivates conservative Christian resistance to same-sex love.

31

LOVE BETWEEN GAYS OR LESBIANS IS WRONG, BECAUSE THE BIBLE TELLS ME SO?

MANY VIEWS ON SEXUALITY AND ONE EXCEPTION

Many anthropological and sociological studies of the tapestry of conservative Christian movements in the United States find not monolithic but complex (and not always consistent) views on gender, sexuality, and family.[3] Far from subscribing to simple and one-dimensional views of the family and relations between the sexes, these Christians have rather complicated views. For example, John Bartkowski and Sally Gallagher find that Evangelical couples have at their disposal a complex framework for understanding and negotiating marital and gender relationships in their everyday life. This variety helps them to anchor their lives in a tradition and at the same time to explore novel modes of being in the world.[4]

Bartkowski shows how advice manuals, sermons, and marriage guides counsel Evangelical couples about various ways to construct the differences between men and women. Some authors allow for a blending of gender roles; others argue for an essential separation of masculine and feminine identity. Likewise, some conservative Christian texts support a strict headship model, in which the husband is the leader of the family. Others propagate the model of the servant–leader, where the husband is both leader and servant of his family. Finally, a minority of Evangelicals read in an egalitarian way the segment of Saint Paul's epistle to the Ephesians, which is the text most often quoted when it comes to gender arrangements within the family: "Now as the Church submits to Christ, so also wives should submit to their husbands in everything. Husbands, love your wives, just as Christ loved the church, and gave himself up for her" (Ephesians 5:21f).

However, there is one topic where for many American Christians the ability to negotiate ambivalence, differences in opinion, and tolerance seemingly comes to an end. This is the issue of how to think religiously about gays, lesbians, and their love. Smith's surveys shows that rejection of such a love is a rare unifying topic among conservative Christians. Moreover this opposition is not only a matter of abstract beliefs, which are pushed by elite ministers, publishers, or lobbyists. It influences how ordinary American Christians relate to their neighbors, fellow congregants, and family members. For example, a similar number of conservative Protestants and other Americans report being bothered by a neighbor of another race. But whereas 38 percent of all Americans would mind having a homosexual as their neighbor, this number rises to 59 percent among those who belong to conservative Christian denominations.[5] In the language of sociology, conservative Christians feel more overt social distance between themselves and homosexuals; said more plainly, the thought of same-sex couples in love makes these Americans very uncomfortable. Why are conservative Christians, who showed an ability to negotiate different gender norms and interpretations of scripture, so rigid when it comes to love between people of the same sex?

This question becomes particularly important if we recall that conservative Christians base their different opinions about gender on conflicting interpretations of the Bible.[6] They relate the various ways of being a Christian couple to different interpretations of the same Bible texts. Again, if conservative Christians have the ability to adjust, change, and vary their ideals about sexuality and gender in the modern world, why do they not use this interpretive skill to find biblical warrants for a Christian acceptance of same-sex love? After all, a minority of Evangelical organizations, such as the group Soulforce, which is led by a former aide of Jerry Falwell, the Rev. Mel White, interpret the biblical texts as accommodating love between Christians of the same sex.[7] Why does the conservative Christian mainstream reject these rival interpretations? And why is homosexuality the topic where an allegedly fluid and nuanced attitude toward sexuality and the Bible becomes brittle?

THE ROLE OF SCRIPTURE IN FORMING BELIEFS ABOUT SEXUALITY

It would be tempting to point to the idea of biblical inerrancy and to say that Evangelical Christians simply have no leeway in interpreting the Word of God, which is believed to be the unfailing truth. As noted earlier, the notion that belief in biblical inerrancy is the key factor in Evangelical attitudes toward sexuality is a staple in the scholarship on conservative Christians.

We should be skeptical about this consensus among both scholars and many conservative Christians alike. It is simplistic to think that Evangelicals go to the Bible to figure out what to think about the love of gays and lesbians, read the text, and find a clear answer.[8] To say conservative Christians believe love among gays and lesbians is sinful because the Bible tells them so begs the question why the rejection of homosexuality is a major unifying theme among them.[9] In the gospel of Mark we find Jesus explicitly proscribing divorce, and yet we don't see Christian conservative organizations lobbying for an adoption ban for divorced people (Mark 10:11, 12). Pointing to a hermeneutic of selective reading does not help either. This strategy leads to the question of why Paul's Letter to the Romans (one of the texts considered proof for the Bible's rejection of homosexual behavior) serves as a public policy statement, but the texts banning divorce do not. In short, claiming that belief in biblical inerrancy explains the rejection of same-sex love makes conservative Christians seem willful and capriciously inconsistent. Instead of taking "the Bible says so" as an answer, let us therefore inquire about what belief in biblical inerrancy means and how it influences conservative Christian attitudes on gender.

Anthropologist Didi Herman describes biblical inerrancy as follows: It "is the belief that the Christian testament, and, to some extent, the Hebrew

Bible are to be taken literally as the word of God. The idea that these documents are to be read in their 'social context' or interpreted in light of changing values is an abomination."[10] A cursory reading of this definition might lead one to believe that for Evangelical Christians inerrancy implies literalism and that they do not interpret the Bible or do not think that they do so. Yet this is clearly not the case. For example, discussing whether masturbation is morally acceptable for boys, the advice columnist for *Breakaway*, a Focus on the Family magazine for young males, writes explicitly that contextual considerations are important in reading the biblical passages that are used to condemn masturbation (Genesis 38:8–11 and 1 Corinthians 6:9–10).[11] Moreover, he cautions that his advice should not contravene what the pastors or parents of his young readers say. Apparently, the columnist acknowledges that Christians have legitimately different opinions and interpretations of biblical evidence when it comes to this topic. And in the countless Bible study groups held all over the country we find that Evangelical Christians do interpret the Bible and that they know that they do so. Advice columnist Candice Watters distinguishes in *Boundless*, another Focus publication, two types of scriptural passages that require special help when interpreting them: obscure texts and those that are in opposition to the current culture, such as the texts condemning homosexuality. She bristles at the idea of always explaining away the message of these contrarian passages with the argument that these parts of the Bible were meant for a different culture, yet Watters acknowledges that sometimes such references to historical context are important, as in the case of explaining why animal sacrifice is not a required performance for Christians.[12] Thus, in texts by conservative Christian organizations such as Focus on the Family, we find awareness that reading the biblical text involves interpretation and an acknowledgment of the scriptural and historical context of a passage.

SUBMISSION TO THE TEXT

This should make us wonder whether Herman's equation of inerrancy with biblical literacy is a correct depiction of how conservative Christians engage the Bible. A meeting of international Evangelical leaders convened by Billy Graham in Lausanne in 1974 affirmed "the divine inspiration, truthfulness and authority" of the entire Bible as the exclusive source of God's revelation. As such the Bible is "without error in all that it affirms and [constitutes] the only infallible rule of faith and practice."[13] The so-called Lausanne covenant rejects the position that the biblical text was somehow corrupted in its historical transmission. Yet this rejection does not imply that literalism should be the overarching strategy in reading the Bible. In fact, even among conservative Christians who subscribe to the belief that the Bible is the unchangeable word of God, there is no clear consensus about which texts should be seen as literally true. For example, not all Christians believe that the earth was indeed created in six twenty-four-hour days or that Jesus will return and rule the earth for exactly one millennium. Reading the biblical text is a more complex activity than the acts of insisting on biblical truth makes it sound. Susan Harding explains this point well in *The Book of Jerry Falwell.* Even if Christians consider the Bible as containing the fixed and unchanging truth of God, they are still confronted with the task of discerning what the Bible means. "The Bible," Harding writes, "is at once a closed canon and open book, still alive, a living Word."[14] Far from uncritical literalism, conservative Christian attitudes toward the Bible are more fluid and (not surprisingly) theologically grounded.

To understand better the role the biblical text is supposed to play in the lives of these Christians and in the formation of their attitude toward gender roles, we need to take a closer look at this implied theology of reading scripture. A closer analysis of the position and importance of the preacher will make clearer how the word of God is considered to be still revealing itself in today's world.

It is a well-known trope among conservative Christians that preachers are to stand in the gap between scripture and the ordinary lives of their audience. This image acknowledges that the preacher has the task, as Harding writes, to turn the biblical text into spoken words.[15] Such a conversion of text to speech presupposes that the preacher actualizes the speaking of the Holy Spirit today. Here is how one of the pastors of Jerry Falwell's Liberty Baptist Church explains to Harding the role of the Spirit in preaching: "There is another agent working while I'm preaching. And he's the Holy Spirit. . . . When I make a statement from the Word of God, and the Holy Spirit bears me up, and he begins to deal with your heart about it, then when we parted company, he's still working."[16]

If conservative Christians talk among themselves or to researchers about the Bible as the Word of God that is guiding their lives, then probably a host of theological tropes works in the background. The Word is a text whose meaning becomes alive through the agency of the Holy Spirit or Jesus, agencies that are notoriously difficult to control. After all, conservative Christians know that, according to Matthew (Mathew 4:3–10), the devil resorts to quoting scripture when he tries to tempt Jesus (namely parts of Psalm 91). Preachers and anyone else who wants to discern the "true" meaning of the biblical text need to speak in such way that the Spirit can work. Such a speech requires that the preacher relinquish power and submit to the divine agent, which is the Spirit. The task is to give "liberty" to its voice and to let him (most Christians imagine the Spirit as somehow male) penetrate one's inner life. The act of reading the Bible with authority requires therefore submission to the powers of Jesus and to letting Jesus dwell in one's inner life. At the same time, this openness presupposes activity: This is the act of letting the Spirit in or of handing oneself over to divine agency. In short, biblical interpretation involves a complex dance of passivity and activity at the right moments.

The idea that the biblical text can be correctly interpreted only with divine help is an old one in Christianity. For example, twelfth-century mystic Rupert from Deutz connects his ability to speak about the Bible to an authorizing vision in which his soul receives the presence of Jesus, as the second person of the Trinity. In this vision a golden substance impregnates what the mystic describes as "the uterus of the inner person" or the "womb of the soul" (*uterum interioris hominis, uterum animae*). Bernard McGinn interprets Rupert's vision as presenting himself as a new Mary birthing the right (i.e., Christological) meaning of scripture.[17]

By mentioning this particular mystic I want to point out that it is not by chance that talking about submission to the text provokes resonances in the registers of gender and sexuality. In historical and contemporary contexts where the right wifely role is connected to a discourse of submission under male authority, it is impossible to avoid such metaphorical crosscurrents. In fact, in the following chapters we will encounter again this resonance between sexual images and the conundrum of agency when it comes to submission to the will of God. That this is not a far-fetched relationship can be seen by Gallagher's conclusion that for Evangelical Christians, ideas about male headship are connected to a theological issue. This is the "right understanding of God the father and source of authority."[18] Submitting oneself to the text, preparing for submission to the voice of God, and having the right kind of submission and activity in one's family life—these are symbolic circles that resonate with one another and reinforce each other. Discourses of gender and sexuality, authority, and theology interconnect.

Later in this book we will explore in detail this network of connections and how it relates to how conservative Christian organizations depict gays and lesbians and their love. For now, let me conclude with the following suggestion: We should not take claims to biblical inerrancy too literally. The Bible is not a text standing outside the lives of conservative Christians. It is part of their lives, and their lives are part of the Bible as living Word. By talking about themselves in biblical images or turns of phrases and by connecting the events of their biographies with the stories of the Bible, readers of this text interweave their own reality with that of their scriptures. This strategy of theological reading allows conservative Christians to acknowledge both the authority of the text and the need for interpretation. They strike a delicate balance between the power of humans and the power of God in the dance of Christian salvation.

WHAT MAKES A TEXT RING TRUE? (SUB)CULTURAL RESONANCES

But how can an individual Christian be sure that her preacher is speaking with the right authority, that is, with the Spirit? There is no claim to an institutional guarantee that the preacher has the right kind of submission to the voice of God, as in the case of the official doctrines of the Roman Catholic Church. There it is taught that a sacramental act of ordination can guarantee that the preacher will speak with the authority of the Holy Spirit. Such a sacramental and institutional safeguard is an alien concept for conservative Christians. Here any Christian, having gained the right interpretive stance toward the biblical text, can speak with authority the word of God into our world. The hallmark of such interpretation therefore is not institutional acknowledgment but the assurance that the Spirit works in the hearts of the congregation.

In other words, it is for the (Spirit-filled) community to judge whether they feel that the preacher is authentically bringing the Word of God to life. The resonances within the community authenticate the preachers, who in turn aim to allow the biblical word to work within their audience. Biblical inerrancy as an interpretive strategy therefore presupposes circuits of relationships between individual readers of the Bible, who consider themselves filled with the Spirit, their communities, and their preachers. The Bible may be seen as the unquestionable authority to guide one's life, yet knowing whether a specific preacher or fellow Christian speaks with biblical authority depends on whether these words resonate as true within the community.

What resonates as true within a given community may not always be clear, and it can change rather quickly. Harding warns that references to the inerrancy of scripture by scholars and practitioners alike should not make us forget that members of a single church can and do subscribe to various interpretations of a given biblical passage. Importantly, she points out that the idea of biblical inerrancy often obscures how quickly such interpretations change or are forgotten, even those promulgated by church officials.[19]

I take Harding's observation not to mean that conservative Christians are mistaken in insisting on the divinely secured inerrancy of the biblical text. Rather, her work can help us to see complexities involved in evoking the unchanging truth of the Bible. To this end she points us to Jerry Falwell's shift in attitude toward the history of racial segregation in the American South. In his autobiography Falwell claims that he saw the unjust nature of segregation during a conversation in 1963 with an elderly African American man, a shoeshine clerk, whom Falwell simply called Lewis. When Lewis asked why he could not join Falwell's church, the preacher had no answer. "I had no reasons, only excuses."[20] Thomas Road Baptist Church did not admit its first black family until 1970. Yet the point of the story is not just to backdate Falwell's embrace of desegregation and thus to gloss over the fact that in his preaching in the 1950s and 1960s he was a vocal supporter of segregationist politics. The rhetorical structure of the story, as Harding points out, is one of biblical conversion. Like the biblical figure of King David "who sinned, was rebuked, and blessed again," Falwell presents himself as receiving the life-changing word of God from a person of lower social status, here the clerk Lewis. Through the conversation with Lewis, Falwell could hear the "small voice of God in his heart" convicting

38

him of being entangled in the injustices of segregation. "I have never once considered myself a racist. Yet, looking back, I have to admit that I was one." Importantly, the injustice of segregation was not a message that he had picked up from his elders: "To the contrary, all my role models, including powerful church leaders, supported segregation."[21]

Indeed, as American historian Jane Dailey writes, there was a broad consensus among Southern white Evangelical Christians that segregation was biblically founded and thus divinely mandated. "Dr. W. M. Caskey, a professor at Mississippi College (the state's leading Baptist institution), explained in 1960, 'We . . . believe with Governor [Ross] Barnett, that our Southern segregation way is the Christian way. . . . [W]e believe that this Bible teaches that Thou wast the original segregationist.'" For many conservative Christians the conviction that God was a segregationist was grounded in what they perceived as the correct reading of the biblical text. It was plain and simple for them that interracial marriage was the sin that God punished in Sodom and that led to the flood or the destruction of the tower of Babel. Or that the second part of Paul's speech in Acts 17:26 meant that God's plan was for each race to live separately. Here we read that God "decreed how long each nation should flourish and what the boundaries of its territory should be." That segregation rests on the biblically warranted divine order for each race to inhabit its divinely allotted territory was an idea of wide appeal.[22]

Harding observes that "as support for segregation gradually eroded during the late 1960s and 1970s, there was no debate about the truth of these Bible verses. They simply stopped being cited. They, or rather their prevailing interpretation which had been considered to be the biblical inerrant truth, ceased to be part of the spoken Bible."[23] Note that it was not exegetical debates discussing the pros and cons of a particular reading of these Bible verses, which allegedly mandated segregation, that brought about this change. Rather, the segregationist reading of these texts ceased to resonate as true with conservative Christians. Only *after* it stopped resonating as true did preachers such as Jerry Falwell claim that the biblical text rejects segregation and slavery.

Yet memories of the widespread Christian support for segregation as a biblically mandated practice surely persisted in Falwell's circles. Therefore he had to shape his conversion narrative against the fact that most leaders of the Church in the 1950s and 1960s saw the Bible as mandating a social policy that Falwell came to consider unjust. In accounting for this reassessment of what the Bible teaches, he aimed to show he was motivated not by political reasons or powers. Not the courts, Congress, or the mass demonstrations changed his heart, wrote Falwell in his autobiography, but "God's still small voice in my heart." The voice of the Spirit must have told him what the right way to read scripture was, in rejection of dominant theological interpretations. In this autobiographical example, references to the inner voice of God justify changes in how to read scripture.

In general, it is not too likely that a strategy of solely discussing alternative interpretations of the biblical passages that allegedly condemn the love of same-sex couples will change conservative Christian attitudes toward gay and lesbian couples. The issue is not to find new information about the biblical text or new exegetical tools for how to read it. Rather, the question is whether conservative Christians are willing to read the text in a more inclusive way. Particularly, it seems that knowing a person who is gay or lesbian has a great impact on whether people change their views.[24] In sum, what is at stake for Christians is the text understood not as a string of letters but as the biblical Word, which is conceived of as authoritative because it resonates as true with the Spirit-filled believers. What establishes these resonances? Why does one reading of the text ring true for conservative Christians whereas another does not?

READING AND BEING EMBEDDED IN A (SUB)CULTURE

According to Gallagher, most influential for the shaping of an Evangelical's belief about sexuality are not "attitudes about the Bible, socioeconomic characteristics, or even geographical location." Rather, her data show that the degree to which a particular respondent is embedded in a particular denomination or Evangelical subculture predicts what Evangelicals think about gender. For example, the hours spent listening to Christian talk radio or other media sources predict better than the professing of belief in biblical inerrancy how a person feels about the appropriate roles for men and women in family and society.[25] The plausibilities of the cultural context in which they live shape how biblical texts resonate for conservative Christians and what they consequently hold to be true about sexuality.

40

They are not capricious in selecting the biblical texts to which they relate their beliefs about gender; rather they react to what strikes them as plausible.

This is not a surprising finding, given how we read texts. Our capacity to understand a word, a joke, or a story depends on our drawing the right connections, using appropriate background knowledge, and supplying the right (or right amount of) information. An observation that literary theorist and novelist Umberto Eco makes in his *Six Walks in the Fictional Woods* can illustrate this point:

> Earlier . . . I cited two fictional passages in which there was a horse and a carriage. The first one, by Achille Campanile, made us laugh because the character Gedeone, asking a coachman to come and pick him up the next day, specified that he ought to bring the coach as well—and by the way, 'Don't forget the horse!' We laughed because it seemed obvious that the horse had to come too, even if it hadn't been mentioned explicitly. We encountered another coach in *Sylvie*: during the night, it takes our narrator toward Loisy. If you read the pages where that journey is described . . . you will see that the horse is never mentioned. So maybe that horse doesn't exist in *Sylvie*, since it doesn't appear in the text? Yet it does exist. While reading, you imagine it trotting through the night, imparting a bumping movement to the carriage, and it is under the physical influence of those soft bumps that the narrator, as if listening to a lullaby, begins once more to dream.[26]

As readers of a text we have to know a great deal about the world, in this case about carriages and horses in late nineteenth-century France. Furthermore, we have to be capable of supplying information that the story requires but does not mention. And we need to know when to stop filling in background knowledge or which connections not to draw and which questions not to ask. Reading presupposes this ability to seemingly naturally expand a text. What we consider to be appropriate background knowledge when reading a text depends on our historical and cultural location. For example, consider how a joke is read as funny in one context but not in another. Whether or how a text resonates with us and how we read it depends on what seems plausible to us, or outrageous, thought provoking, mundane, and so on.

Gallagher's contention that it is not an abstract doctrinal belief in biblical authority that shapes a person's belief about sexuality and gender, but the degree to which she is embedded in a specific (sub)culture, is therefore not surprising. It shows that at stake in the debates about marriage is not the Bible per se (as an abstract thing) but cultural assumptions about sexuality or about the place of men and women in family and nation. Any discussions of biblical evidence for or against gay or lesbian sex therefore entail examining the wider religious and political resonances that are at play when scripture is read.

A CONFLUENCE OF FORCES: RELIGION AND POLITICS

At this point we encounter another potentially misleading explanation for how conservative Christians shape their opinions about sexuality: Politics, and not religion, shapes what Americans think about same-sex love, because doctrinal belief about the inerrancy of the Bible is not the deciding factor in forming conservative Christian opinion. The scholar who argues this point most forcefully is sociologist of religion Alan Wolfe. He also raises the objection that ordinary Americans are not influenced by the output of conservative Christian elite media organizations. Instead of being proponents of theological conservatism, American Evangelicals are actually religious innovators and make up the more mobile segments of the U.S. population today. According to Wolfe, Evangelicals are not theologically conservative but innovative, yet they are politically conservative, and their rejection of same-sex love is a reflection of the latter and not the former attitude. This position deserves a detailed treatment, because Wolfe's argument presupposes a clear distinction between the religious and the political. Moreover, he seems to assume that religious revivalism and conservatism are two different things. Here is where it is helpful to look at scholarship about the political and religious revivals in South Asia. We will see that the revivalist Buddhist or Hindu leaders whom we will encounter reject both religious and political elites and argue for a revitalized religion and state. They see themselves as innovators and as preservers of tradition. Understanding the interaction between the political and the religious languages used in these revivals is central not only for the analysis of our particular debate about sexuality. Learning from the examples of South Asian politics will help us to gain a deeper assessment of how religious interests originate and function in our polity.

Thus, I will spend some time tracing the connection between political and religious motives in the language about same-sex love. In the remainder of this chapter I will do this in three steps: First I will use Alan Wolfe's work to present and critique the argument that political interests are at issue and not religious ones. Second, I will turn to a dispute between Wolfe and James Hunter about the influence of religious values and elite producers of culture on ordinary Americans. We will therefore see that the interactions between elite producers of conservative Christian culture and ordinary Christians do not follow the script of political elites duping ordinary religious people. Rather, I will show that a religious and political reimagination of the culture of American politics is played out in our debates. We then can ask, "What ideas about same-sex love, America, and religion do the languages circulated by elite producers of conservative Christian culture present as plausible?" Addressing this question in the remaining chapters will help us understand how and why this elite discourse resonates with the wider American public. Third, we will see how in this language religious revival, references to tradition, and political conservatism interact. Connecting this analysis with a look at other religious and political revival movements will fasten the link between the political and the religious realm. The context in which the Bible is read is therefore defined by a web of interacting political, sexual, and religious concerns. Disentangling this web is the task of the remaining chapters of this book.

FAMILY VALUES AS OPIUM FOR THE PEOPLE?

The argument that religious language only clouds ulterior political motives appears in one form in Tom Frank's popular book *What Is the Matter with Kansas?*[27] Frank claims that Republican strategists and their organizational network mobilize a rhetorical barrage of appeals to family, to America's Christian character, and to so-called biblical values. They do this not for religious concerns but to push an economic and legislative agenda that privileges the rich and powerful. In this manner, Republicans create a rhetorical machine aimed at fashioning an electoral majority for political goals from which only a minority of voters will benefit. Endorsing Frank's analysis, Wolfe argues that Republicans mobilized the issue of gay marriage only during the 2000 and 2004 election cycles. In contrast, in the immediate aftermath of the elections the real work of governance, such as the mundane issues of financial and Social Security reform, took center stage of Republican political activity.[28]

According to this position, the frenzied debates surrounding marriage for gays and lesbians are whipped up for day-to-day political goals. And indeed, the election year in 2004 produced a spike in the number of Americans rejecting same-sex marriage. In that year we saw a sharp reversal of the decade-long movement toward greater acceptance of legalizing same-sex marriage or domestic partnerships. In 2006, these numbers continued to follow the long-term trend by showing for the first time a majority endorsing domestic partnership legislation. It seems as if the spigot of religiously expressed resistance against marriage for people of the same sex can be turned on and off, according to the political needs of the day. Wolfe argues that whereas the Republican machine uses religion to obscure its ulterior (economic) motives, Democratic voters seem less motivated by religious intangibles. They are more informed about and interested in particular policy positions. Wolfe states that during the 2004 election, these voters were more able to identify the policy positions of their candidates than Republican voters. And he concludes "that one side was motivated more by policy and the other by intangibles, like character."[29] This finding squares with the observation that individual voters use references to biblical values to express political motivations that are difficult for them to put into words.

Thus, one can indeed wonder whether religious concerns are at stake or whether religious language is the cover for something else, such as the intangible issues that many Republican voters themselves have difficulty expressing. Let me recall the previously mentioned odd finding of the Pew study about the motivations of Americans who reject legitimizing marriage between people of the same sex. As I noted in chapter 1, the Pew researchers asked these respondents about their reasons for so doing. If asked in an open-ended format, which allowed the respondents to answer freely what came to their minds, roughly 45 percent presented reasons that the Pew researchers identified as "religious" in a broad sense. (The Pew report mentions the following categories into which they organized the responses: "It is a sin," "it is morally wrong," "the Bible says so" formed one category, and "it is against my religious belief" another). If asked in this an open format, only 1 percent replied that allowing gays or lesbians to marry would undermine the traditional family. Given the prevalence of this argument in the rhetorical battles against gay and lesbian marriage, this low number is surprising. Even more surprising is what happened when the Pew researchers changed the format when asking Americans about why they opposed marriage for gays and lesbians. When the question was asked in a format that required the interviewees to select from a menu of options, then 56 percent of all Americans and fully 76 percent of all those who oppose marriages for people of the same sex agreed that "gay marriage would undermine the traditional family."[30] Moreover, 62 percent of all Americans and 82 percent of opponents of such marriages stated that legitimizing them would go against their religious beliefs. It seems as if religious language allows Americans to mold otherwise diverse or intangible sentiments into a coherent set of "religious" reasons. Thus, one might be compelled to argue that not religious values but some other intangible issues motivate conservative American Christians in their rejection of same-gender marriage.

The problem with this argument is that it disjoins religious and political languages and ideas. Political scientists may focus on how politicians use religious language to build coalitions and to further their own goals. Yet why do some Americans feel that religious language expresses things that they cannot put into words in other ways? Politicians can use religiously loaded language only if they think it resonates with the people they hope to reach. Finally, what is the role of the conservative Christian media organizations and churches that produce and disseminate a ceaseless stream of radio programs, videos and CDs, booklets, Internet sites, sermons on tape, and the like? Are they just doing the work of politicians? The consumers of their products would not agree with this characterization. A substantial number of conservative Christians critique organizations of the so-called Christian Right as being too political.[31] Thus it makes sense that Focus on the Family claims that it is not involved in partisan politics. This group battles for American values, for America's children, and for the Christian character of the nation, but Dobson denies being a politician.

THE LANGUAGE OF ELITES AND OF ORDINARY
CONSERVATIVE CHRISTIANS

To examine this connection between political and religious language, let us take a closer look at the relationship between so-called elite producers of Christian language and the consumers of their media products. In particular, let me consider a recent debate between sociologists James Hunter and Alan Wolfe about the influence of conservative Christians in politics. For Hunter the debates about opening marriage to gays and lesbians and about other matters of sex and public policy indicate a deeper conflict in American society. True, these debates are conducted mainly by elite actors, that is, those who have access to the production of media (from sermons and leaflets to Internet portals), and by a small yet energized group of grassroots activists. Yet these elites shape in important ways the prevailing values and norms found in our society, according to Hunter. They form culture through the production of a shared language, through which we experience ourselves and the world.[32]

According to Hunter, the elites who shape the wider public's linguistic options and the grassroots activists who disseminate the elite views are engaged in a battle over the culture of American politics. With this term he means the broader values and visions that characterize America. The "war" over what is the right culture of politics for America is fought on numerous battlefields throughout the United States on issues ranging from school prayer, to Terri Schiavo, to marriage for people of the same sex. Yet in all these conflicts Hunter detects two alternative moral visions that are at the heart of what he sees as the present-day culture wars: traditionalism and progressivism.

Traditionalists are not simply reactionaries. Rather, in engaging the issues of the present day, they seek a deliberate continuity with the "ordering principle inherited from the past." Progressives, on the other hand, see these inherited principles as only partially useful and more often than not as tools legitimizing oppression. They turn to a measured way of experimentation and innovation. Underlying this distinction is a marked difference in how the ultimate reality that legitimizes social action is perceived. Traditionalists subscribe to the idea that there is an "ultimate reality that is rooted in transcendent authority," says Hunter; progressives claim that "what is real or good is not so much constant and enduring but rather much more personal and dependent on the particularities of the context."[33]

Although the culture war is fought by a small minority of elites and their activists, a large number of Americans are not passive bystanders. Rather, Hunter finds that roughly 25 percent of Americans form a traditionalist or neo-traditionalist camp. (Hunter claims that the latter differs from the former because of their urban residence and access to better education). They proclaim theistic beliefs and a "commitment to traditional morality, self-sacrifice, and a belief in absolutes." Another 25–27 percent, who mostly are lenient in relation to traditional morality and relativistic toward truth, belong to the permissivist camp, according to Hunter. These Americans show less willingness to sacrifice personal interest for the common good, says Hunter.[34] Instead of detecting a vital center of Americans who hold measured and pragmatic views, Hunter claims that slightly more than half of all Americans can be mobilized by liberal or conservative elites. Issues of religion provide the motivating force for these mobilizations. For Hunter, religious identity is not defined by denominational differences (i.e., whether one is Catholic or Jewish). Rather, whether a person perceives the world as a traditionalist or a progressive will predict how she votes or what her stance will be on issues such as marriage for same-sex couples.

Because Alan Wolfe thinks that political and not religious concerns are at stake, he claims that the debate about so-called cultural issues is primarily an elite preoccupation, that is, one of politicians, media makers, and the like. The interests of the political elites keep alive the intense debates about abortion, marriage for gays and lesbians, and so on. Ordinary Americans resent these conflicts, as the reactions to the case of Terri Schiavo showed.[35] Underlying this first argument is another claim: that the disagreements that shape American politics are political, not religious. They are debates between conservatives and liberals in a political sense, not between those who are religiously conservative or liberal. Here his main point is that Evangelicals, who are politically conservative, are religious innovators. Before we discuss this point, let us examine Wolfe's first argument that the debates about same-sex love are mostly an elite preoccupation.

The statistical findings of Gallagher and Smith and the in-depth interviews of Harding reveal evidence to the contrary. Conservative Christians

47

respond positively to the language they hear (e.g., on their radio stations), and this language can galvanize what they think about love between people of the same sex. In the discussion of the relationship between preachers and their communities we found that the preacher's words needed to resonate as true with the ordinary Christian and their own experiences of the world. The so-called elite producers of language and the ordinary consumers of it interact in a community-forming exchange of words.

Wolfe is correct in focusing on what ordinary people actually think and sense to be true. He does not want to talk about culture as its own structure independent of the choices ordinary citizens make.[36] If we think, as Hunter does, that language is one of the conduits through which cultural values are established and reinforced, then Wolfe is surely right. It is not the structures of language that determine (somehow independently of how we speak) what people mean to say with their words and how they experience and categorize the world. Rather, people speak, and they appropriate, nuance, alter, innovate, or forget the codes of acceptable speech they have inherited. Attention to the inherited structures of language or culture should not overshadow this ability of speakers to innovate, as Wolfe correctly observes; yet we should not downplay the fact that individual speakers are not completely free to alter or reject the language (or culture) they inhabit. Russian literary theorist Michael Bakhtin argues that "language is not a neutral medium that passes freely and easily into the private property of the speaker's intention; it is populated, overpopulated—with the intentions of others."[37] We are not free to reinterpret or change the inherited language as if it were our private possession, which is an important point Wolfe overlooks.

Conservative Christians use language that is already filled with the intentions of others, namely the preachers, authors, media producers, and fellow believers who make up their communities. The ordinary Christians Harding describes "join a narrative tradition, a way of knowing and being through storytelling" and through sharing of stories.[38] While they contribute to this tradition they also have to embed themselves and their own stories into it by following the patterns of language that this tradition values. Anthropological studies of authors such as Melanie Griffith, who like Wolfe focuses on the language use of ordinary Christians, show how elite discourse influences their understanding of self and world. Despite the multiplicity of linguistic patterns (e.g., prayers, devotional texts, advice manuals, hymns),

Griffith acknowledges that the "tradition" itself aims at limiting the range of possible interpretations. Only certain stories can be selected for retelling, and only certain understandings of these stories are validated by repetition and proliferation.[39]

Wolfe might contest that people, not traditions, do the limiting, and this is an important point. The elaborate methods of persuasion, reinforcement, and discipline of speech happen through the mediation of people who are in a position to shape (if not completely control) what counts as appropriate language. In Hunter's picture these are the elite producers of culture, the media organizations, preachers, pamphleteers, and women and men in any community able to censor and encourage certain forms of speech.

Moreover, Griffith points out that ordinary Christians reinforce the widely circulating scripts of gender and sexuality when they retell their own stories with the help of the narrative patterns produced by the elites. We need not succumb to the fiction that these patterns have their own dynamics and simply force ordinary people to speak and think in certain ways.[40] Yet claiming that elites have no power to constrain what Christians think is clearly implausible as well. Thus Hunter's concern with the wider culture in which political choices are made seems valid, and his focus on what he calls the culture of politics makes sense.

Yet Wolfe is right in rejecting Hunter's aim to find the deep structure of culture. With this term Hunter refers to the wider symbolic context in which we engage with political decision making and institutions. Recalling what the horses in Umberto Eco's anecdote have taught us about the importance of background knowledge for the understanding any story, we can say the following: Hunter's *deep structure* refers to the right kind of background knowledge and attitudes that we all bring to the analysis of and action within our political contexts.[41]

However, I don't think talking about a singular deep structure is helpful in thinking about language or culture. Rather, using the words of Griffith, we might say that Hunter is pointing to the narrative scripts that constrain how we use, with variations, our words. And here we must note that not everyone has an equal capacity to introduce such narrative patterns or successfully circulate them into the wider public. We can see church communities—with their ability to repetitively shape language in each church service—and the various media outlets as powerful elite institutions that form and distribute

49

narrative scripts. These scripts may not add up to a single superstructure that determines the character of our culture. Yet multiple narrative scripts and fragments thereof can shape what Wittgenstein calls a form of life, that is, a network of plausibilities within and against which we act in and think about the world. Every day we make decisions that reflect our shared cultural assumptions. These acts or thoughts seem completely natural to us, such as greeting someone in the elevator, driving carefully so that we don't violate the traffic laws, or suppressing a laugh at a joke that we deem inappropriate. There is no superstructure that makes us act this way; rather, these practices are simply plausible for us. Yet it would be difficult to explain these decisions to someone who is alien to our form of life. Why do you greet someone in one way and not another? Do we really believe that humans have free will, and if we don't, why can I not use this conviction as a defense in traffic court? And how do you explain how a joke can be both funny and inappropriate?

Wittgenstein's idea of forms of life is better suited to the fragmentary nature of our shared plausibilities than Hunter's concept of deep structure. Instead of a single clearly demarcated structure we find a web of practices, institutions, and narratives. The stories we tell ourselves and others about America in general (or rural Vermont specifically), the buildings we build with private bathrooms and sleeping arrangements, the paperwork we fill out to get a marriage license or job, our institutions of government, our media outlets, our shopping malls: all these shape what we consider to be plausible or natural or appropriate.

Where does our discussion of Wolfe's first thesis lead us? Rejecting his idea that elite discourses do not affect how ordinary Americans think or act allows us to inquire into the following: Which ideas about lesbians and gays, America, and religion are presented as plausible in the narrative scripts circulated by elite producers of conservative Christian culture? Addressing this question will help us understand how and why this elite discourse resonates with the wider American public.

What about Wolfe's more basic argument that the elite producers of conservative Christian culture are not religiously but politically conservative? Against Hunter's typology, Wolfe argues that Evangelical Christians, for example, are not "traditional" in a traditional sense. Most of them do not live in traditional families, but many have experienced divorce, and they do not simply continue their religious heritage but have explicitly rejected their past religious affiliation, in the case of born-again Christians.

Instead of seeing conservatives mostly as ardent defenders of truth, we should acknowledge that they are seekers who belong to the most mobile segments of the American population: They remarry, change employment, move from one part of the country to another, and many times also change their faith communities with these moves. In contrast, liberals live in much more traditional settings, says Wolfe. The divorce rates in Massachusetts are much lower than those in Oklahoma, for example, and liberal liturgical practices are much more in line with historical precedent. Liberals have pipe organs in their churches, as Wolfe points out.[42]

He acknowledges that his descriptions verge on caricature, but his point has merit. Wolfe finds that conservative Christians as a whole are not interested in doctrinal rigor. Traditional theology is less important than getting the music right and making visitors feel welcome. To spread the gospel, Evangelicals rely on any cultural innovation available (from the Internet to modern music styles). Overall, Wolfe finds that conservative Christians are not focused on sinfulness but rather endorse a confident message about unlocking the full human potential.[43] Talk about sin, which Wolfe considers an essential theological feature of traditional Evangelical Christianity, has been transformed into a discourse of self-help. Traditional religion, understood as adherence to traditional doctrinal belief systems, is not a deciding factor in American politics, Wolfe implicitly argues. Contemporary conservative Christians are not faithful stewards of a theology handed down by their forebears. Theological continuity in this sense is not an issue for them. Yes, much of present-day Evangelical theology is historically connected to Puritan versions of Calvinist theology. But this does not mean that Evangelical pastors are interested in preserving the right kind of Calvinism.

To sum up Wolfe's argument: First, the new mega-churches and conservative denominations are not religious in this traditional sense. Though politically conservative, they are religious inventors. And second, Wolfe insists "that our differences are political rather than cultural or religious; we disagree over abortion or gay marriage because some of us are conservatives and others liberals, not because some of us are religious and others secular."[44]

Wolfe assumes that (besides having pipe organs in a church) adhering to and continuing faithfully a lineage of theological orthodoxy is the only way in which one can be religiously traditional or conservative. Yet the story is more complicated. For example, the Christians interviewed by Griffith and Gallagher find it important that their ideas about sexuality and about God are not innovations. Rather, for them such beliefs reflect a divinely ordered world of hierarchies. Gallagher quotes the following statement by Women in Leadership at Calvary Chapel:

> This idea of authority and submission to authority are so important to God that they are part of His very being. The First Person of the Holy Trinity is called the Father; the Second Person of the Holy Trinity is called the Son. Inherent in those titles is a relationship of authority and submission to authority. The Father exercises authority over the Son, and the Son submits to the Father's authority and this is the very nature and being of GOD![45]

These Christians see themselves not as religious innovators but as preserving something that is eternally truthful. (It is not surprising that those holding more egalitarian views of gender argue similarly by using as authoritative the inner life of the Trinity.)

This eternal truth is often equated with the "old-time" religion that folksy shows such as the late Jerry Falwell's *Old Time Gospel Hour* evoke. Consider the exhibit honoring James Dobson in Focus on the Family's visitors' center in Colorado Springs. During a visit in 2006 I saw on display a reddish jacket called the "Christmas Coat." This coat belonged to Dobson's father, who, according to the exhibit, was a gifted painter but gave up his art to become a minister. We are informed that the younger Dobson used to wear this coat every Christmas in memory of his father. With this piece the exhibit not only shows the younger Dobson's devotion to his father but also makes a point about the importance of rooting oneself in wholesome family traditions. Focus stresses the importance of traditional values, which, we are told, are based in the Bible and thus in what is called the Judeo-Christian worldview. These values are presented as not resulting from contemporary innovations, against which Focus on the Family rallies its conservative Christian followers.[46] Theirs is not an unproblematic evocation of the past; rather, we find a sense that today's world is disconnected from the timeless biblical wisdom that founds the Judeo-Christian ethic and traditional values. What was good and old is juxtaposed with a present that is perceived as new and bad.

A telling example of this invocation of a better past in the face of a problematic present is a story titled "A Heartwarming Christmas," published as a letter from Dobson on one of Focus's Web sites. This narrative weaves together advice about family, a story about giving, a prayer, and a call to respect Christianity and the sacrifices that must be made for the nation. After recalling an exceedingly hot battle for biblical values and the institution of the family in 2004, Dobson admonishes us to read the gospel of Christ's birth. Then we are transported back into a story about a wholesome American neighborhood, told as the memory of a little boy who grew up to become a leader in Focus's ministry. Together with the young boy narrating the tale, we meet one of the neighbors, a man who joined the Marine Corps at age sixteen to fight in World War II. He decorates his house with Christmas lights, reminding us and the young man that "the miracle of America is worth dying for." Farmer Fred sells Christmas trees, Sister Rosemary teaches the children, and three poor widows are about to receive a Christmas tree. We learn that Christmas is about giving and that in this neighborhood people look out for each other. Like *The Andy Griffith Show*, which illuminates the black and white TV screens in the story, the narrative imagines a wholesome America, before the cultural upheavals of the 1960s. In this narrative, which takes more from Frank Capra's *It's a Wonderful Life* than Mel Gibson's *Passion of the Christ*, religious imagery is deeply embedded in how Dobson wants America to be. As a matter of course, the good American town is suffused with Christian values and symbols. The miracle of Christmas and that of America are intertwined.

Wolfe is therefore right that Evangelicals and conservative Christians (and this means elites such as Falwell as well as the ordinary women Gallagher interviewed) have a complex notion of tradition. It encompasses a sense of both timeless values and the moral decay that characterizes contemporary society, in contrast to a not-so-distant past. In Wolfe's understanding, where the division between religious innovation and tradition is clearly marked, these references to the old times must be considered only a veneer. Thus, Wolfe seems to echo a sentiment expressed by Karl Marx: "Just when people seem engaged in revolutionizing themselves and things [sich und die

53

Dinge umzuwälzen], in creating something entirely new, . . . they anxiously conjure up the spirits of the past to their service and borrow from them names, battle slogans and costumes in order to present the new scene of world history in this time-honored disguise and borrowed language."[47] For Marx these vestiges of old symbols are hindrances to true progress, whereas for Wolfe references to the past seem inconsequential in terms of religion. Yet the relationship between political and religious innovation and conservatism is more complicated than either Marx or Wolfe would allow.

RAPID CHANGE AND APPEALS TO AN AUTHENTIC PAST IN POLITICS AND RELIGION: A GLANCE AT BUDDHIST AND HINDU REVIVALS

Interestingly, when it comes to religion and politics, the "contradictory situation of simultaneous rapid change and frenetic appeals to an 'authentic' past" is not an exclusively American phenomenon.[48] In fact, these contradictions shape what counts as true religion in many instances in the modern period, as we can learn from recent scholarship on the emergence of modern Buddhism, Hinduism, and Islam in the nineteenth and twentieth centuries. For example, in *Buddhism Betrayed?* Stanley Tambiah traces Sri Lanka's present-day conflicts back to the Buddhist revival movements that reimagined both Buddhism and Sri Lankan politics. This political and religious revival was carried mostly by an emerging middle class interested in creating a Sri Lankan national identity against the British colonial oppressors. An exceedingly influential figure in this movement was charismatic Buddhist leader Anagarika Dharmapala (1864–1933).

Important for our discussion is that Dharmapala's goal was to give Buddhism a new vitality in the face of changing political and economic realities. This meant not only rejecting practices that were considered previously unproblematic (such as the use of magic or of certain rituals) but also grounding the renewal in alternative readings of the Buddhist canon and other formative texts. Not surprisingly we find in this Buddhist revival a new construction of an ideal Sri Lankan past as harboring the authentic "Buddhist way of life." This was an immensely important concept in both anticolonial and national rhetoric. References to the "Buddhist way of life" were used to critique the moral lapses of the British colonial powers and the English-educated Sinhalese elites. They also represented "a positive

effort to sketch a mode of life that claims to draw on timeless values en-
shrined in early Buddhism, but which also incorporates traditional features
associated with precolonial rural Sinhala life."[49] Despite this idealization of
the village, an urban-based and educated middle class together with a
young population of Buddhist monks carried the renewal process against
the previously powerful religious elites. And importantly, part of this religious and political struggle was the emergence of a puritanical sexual code
of conduct for the new urban middle-class families. In sum, we see in this
case a complex field of political, religious, cultural, and economic forces
that shape what counts as authentically Buddhist as well as Sri Lankan.
It is important to note that this religious and nationalist revival understands itself both as retrieving a lost past in the face of a denigrated present
and as reinvigorating and innovating the contemporary practice of a timeless tradition.[50]

I mention the case of Dharmapala's Buddhist revival not because I want
to say that Dobson is an American or Christian version of the Sri Lankan
reformer. However, we can learn the following from Tambiah's analysis of
the Buddhist revival: Claims to traditional values (both religious and political) and to religious revitalization and innovation can go hand in hand.
And as Charles Hallisey, another scholar of Sri Lankan Buddhism, cautions, it is not quite the case that these religious innovations are without
grounding in the tradition. The new reading practices, for example, which
made possible Dharmapala's selective reading of the vast Buddhist ca-
nonical literature, were influenced by European models but could also be
connected to previous monastic practices.[51] Thus, the scripturalism that according to Tambiah characterizes Dharmapala's vision of Buddhism can be
seen as being rooted in historical precedent *and* as resulting from religious
innovation. One cannot deny that Dharmapala was indeed revitalizing
historical Buddhism; he was not just creating his own version of it. Although
another Buddhist may argue that Dharmapala got it wrong, the scholar of
religion can perhaps point to changes in how practitioners interact with
their texts. Yet she cannot argue that therefore the Buddhism of the Sri
Lankan revival is inauthentic or not in line with traditional Buddhism.

However, the scholar could conceivably claim that revivalists, like Dharmapala, who use the language of tradition are not really religious actors. They
are political figures who have no claim to religious authenticity. And this is

indeed the route that Wolfe seems to take with respect to Dobson and Falwell when he characterizes them as "media figures."[52] Yet, this strategy overlooks precisely the interesting entanglement of political and religious forces in shaping both political and religious reality that Tambiah's work has laid bare.

In particular, Wolfe prevents us from seeing how in these revivals a new religious elite hopes to establish itself as harbingers of true religion. Thus, religious authenticity is not something that is simply there, a characteristic that the sociologist could measure; rather, it is the result and object of contestations. Another scholar of colonial and postcolonial politics, Partha Chatterjee, describes this dynamic well for the case of the emerging Indian national identity. He notes that before the explicitly political struggle for the establishment of a sovereign state, we find a movement to imagine a shared Indian cultural identity. The supremacy of the British colonizers was acknowledged in the material domain encompassing the economy, the law, science, technology, and statecraft. Yet in the spiritual sphere of school, language, and family the essential markers of true Bengali identity were created. This was considered the space where the true superiority of Bengali culture became evident. A unified Bengali language, a sense of a shared history using European historiographic models, and a new organization of the roles of men and women in the family emerge.[53]

Two points from Chatterjee's discussion are particularly important for our topic. First, we see a change in how the history of Bengal is conceived, with a new focus on what was considered the classical period of Indian and Hindu history. These new and explicitly Bengali histories repeat over and over again a story of a glorious Hindu past, the decline of India under Muslim rule, and the prospect of national cultural and political restoration. Contributing to this history were "all the prejudices of the European Enlightenment about Islam [such as the] stereotypical figure of 'the Muslim' endowed with 'national character': fanatical, bigoted, warlike, dissolute, and cruel." In contrast, the nascent Indian nation was envisioned as fulfilling the promises of classical Hindu culture. A number of religious renewal movements, such as the Brahmo reform movement, related well to this attention to what the new rising middle class perceived as classical Hinduism.[54] And these reformers presented themselves as reviving the authentic truths of Indian religion, which had been lost in times of political and religious decay. In short, a religious revival movement engages in a specific retrieval of the past (under the influence of European cultural forms and political oppression) and thereby shapes political identity, or the "culture of politics" in Hunter's terms.

Second, women were seen as the primary bearers of this classical Hindu spirituality, thus representing the virtues of the nation; the loss of these virtues was greatly feared. "Women . . . must not lose their essentially spiritual (that is, feminine) virtues; they must not in other words become essentially Westernized." Thus, the separation of social roles demanded that women be different from men, particularly within the space of the family. Yet it was also important that the new Bengali woman differentiate herself from both Western and "coarse, sexual, unrefined" lower-class women.[55] Because the bearers of the new Bengali Hindu national identity were members of the rising bourgeoisie, middle-class women had to represent in dress, eating habits, and social relations the superior Bengali culture. We find, perhaps unsurprisingly, that women were meant to adhere to typical middle-class values such as thrift, discipline, and self-control, values that were clearly influenced by Victorian ideals of how to lead a proper life. However, standing in for the ideal India also demanded that the women submit themselves to a religious idealization. Glossing over the real power differences between men and women, we find an ideology that demands

the adulation of women as goddess or as mother. Whatever its source in the classical religions of India or in medieval religious practices, the specific ideological form in which we know the "Indian woman" construct in the modern literature and arts in India today is wholly and undeniably a product of the development of a dominant middle-class culture coeval with the era of nationalism. It served with all the force of mythological inspiration what had in any case become a dominant characteristic of femininity in the new construct of "woman" standing as a sign for "nation," namely the spiritual qualities of self-sacrifice, benevolence, devotion, religiosity, and so on. . . . In fact, the image of woman as goddess or mother, served to erase her sexuality in the world outside the home.[56]

These constructions of the Indian woman again show the contradictory movement of drawing on traditional sources to shape new sexual, religious, and political identities.

What does this mean for our project of understanding conservative Christian concerns about same-sex love? Let me summarize three points that will help us in thinking about religion, politics, and their interrelations in the American context: First, these revival movements aim to reinvigorate what they consider decaying religious traditions by bringing to the fore their timeless truths that were still alive and well in previous (better) times. Thus the idea that a religious movement is either traditional or innovative is oversimplified. Yes, these movements reject the religious status quo, but they do so with the explicit desire to retrieve what they consider the eternal truth of their tradition. If, like Wolfe, we are concerned about the self-understanding of a religious movement, then we need to take these references to tradition seriously.

Second, we see in these cases how difficult it is to distinguish neatly between political and religious narratives. The invocation of traditional religious values was essential for the formation of Sinhalese and Indian nationalisms. As Tambiah writes, the "very conceptualization, phenomenological basis, and practical realization [of Sinhala nationalism] were inseparable from the identity and historical pride provided by the Buddhist legacy, the cultural capital that Buddhist projects generated, and the languages in which Buddhist literature were couched and transmitted."[57] Religious narratives are essential in these cases to shape what Hunter calls the culture of politics. Thus, these insights from contemporary postcolonial theory can echo what political philosopher Michael Oakeshott writes, as Hunter quotes approvingly: "A political system presupposes a civilization. . . . Political activity may have given us the Magna Carta and the Bill of Rights, but not the contents of these documents, which came from a stratum of social thought far too deep to be influenced by the actions of politicians."[58] We may bracket Oakeshott's insistence that politicians cannot influence the webs of practices that shape our forms of life. Yet Chatterjee's examples showed how political institutions (such as the legislature and the judiciary) presupposed the prior production of a shared form of life. Thus before we come together as free citizens to exercise our right to speech and deliberation, we are shaped by narratives that envision and hope to produce a common culture.

Third, these new economic and political demands shaped and were in turn formed by a specific form of religious revival, one that was carried by the nascent middle classes. A new middle-class religion took form in explicit contrast to the religious practices of the hitherto dominant elites, who were derided as ineffectual because of their lack of resistance against the colonial regime or as corrupt because of their collaboration with it. Consequently, new religious authorities appear, and middle-class lay people who did not attend established institutions of religious learning make claims about religious authenticity. Oliver Roy makes a similar argument for contemporary Islam. Religion is conceived as being based in faith and authentic experience and not in long learning or academic seminary training. True religious knowledge is easily accessible if conveyed by a charismatic leader. Religious identity is performed by wearing the right kind of clothes or adopting a specific style of speaking.[59] Although these revivalist religious movements reject the old elites (or orthodoxies, as Chatterjee calls them), they are nevertheless traditionalists in their invocations of a past in which their religion was lived authentically.

Taking a cue from these three points, we should therefore take seriously that conservative Christian narrative scripts about marriage invoke concerns for both the political and the religious character of America. Hunter's claim seems very true, namely that these religious narratives (e.g., about marriage for same-sex couples) imply an attempt to reshape the culture of American politics.

In sum, I wish to interpret the field of religious, sexual, and national themes in the narratives of conservative Christians not as the strategic use of religion for political goals. Politicians of different stripes may aim at building lasting coalitions of different segments of American society by using religious language and aligning themselves to certain Christian lobbying networks. But treating the producers and consumers of religious language in the public sphere simply as pawns in a game of politics obscures the fact that genuine religious concerns are at stake in the debates about same-sex love. In contrast, I will argue that what we see in the religiously charged debates about this love are intricate interactions between religious, sexual, and political ideals and imaginations. Yet we have to tread carefully. We cannot simply adopt, without further discussion, insights gleaned from the political involvement of modern Buddhism or Hinduism for our discussion. However, these insights can give us guiding questions. In the debates about gays and lesbians, how do religious concerns interact with political issues?

What shapes what counts religiously and politically as "traditional" marriage? How do assumptions about "nation" and middle-class concerns enter into American views about religion? In short, we need to clarify how religious, political, and sexual narratives interact in the United States. Chapter 3 will address these questions by taking a closer look at the theological and political history of American debates about marriage.

3

AMERICA AND THE STATE OF
RESPECTABLE CHRISTIAN ROMANCE

In the previous chapter I argued that conservative Chris-
tian narratives about same-sex couples and their love are motivated not simply by a doctrinal belief in biblical literalism or by exclusively political concerns. Rather, we saw how cultural and hence political contexts shape how Christians read the Bible and how they conceive of its truth. And we learned that evocations of tradition in religious revival movements are aimed at rejecting the interpretations of previous elites and endorsing new religious and political regimes. Religious convictions are therefore public and political. They are produced in a political process, and they shape it. Therefore analyzing the fine points of biblical texts without reference to the context of their political use will not be helpful for understanding what is at stake for conservative Christians, nor will treating conservative Christian groups as yet another type of political pressure group. Rather, we have to examine the confluence of political and religious forces in America that shape both political and religious convictions about appropriate forms

61

of sexual behavior in state and family. This is the goal of the present chapter. To this end, I will first turn to what conservative Christian organizations say about allowing marriage for same-sex couples.

SAME-SEX COUPLES AND THE MORAL AND SPIRITUAL STAMINA OF THE NATION

On a frequently asked questions Web site to which Focus on the Family links, Peter Sprigg from the Family Research Council describes three key arguments against allowing same-sex couples to marry. The first argument relies on the definition of marriage and the second on the allegedly harmful nature of same-sex erotic relationships. Because the essential definition of marriage is the union of one man and one woman, Sprigg argues, same-sex unions cannot rightfully be called marriage. Such a definitional argument is weak. "Why not change the definition?," one could argue. Therefore his second claim is that relationships between partners of the same sex are detrimental to our society. Third, like Dobson, Sprigg argues that the meaning of marriage is not anchored in specific legal arrangements but reflects an institution grounded in human nature. Marriage predates the American Constitution in particular and all human law in general.[1]

Sprigg continues by claiming that "reproduction is a central (even if not obligatory) part of the social significance of marriage."[2] Let me note the curious choice of words in this formulation. Calling reproduction an essential and obligatory feature of marriage would establish an interest in letting only couples marry who are able or likely to reproduce. Focus does not seem to go quite that far. Yes, childless marriages are of less interest to the state, says Sprigg, yet to tie marriage too closely to procreation would force the state to intrude too deeply into the heterosexual couple's privacy. Interestingly, we find the emphasis on procreation in marriage only in the context of articles that denounce opening the institution to same-sex couples.

The reason for the curious role of reproductive sex in these arguments is the following: In contrast to official Roman Catholic theology, for example, for most Protestant denominations, being able and willing to engage in procreative sex is not essential for the validity of a marriage. Marriage is the necessary context for morally acceptable procreative sex, but procreative sex is not necessary for a morally appropriate marriage.

If reproduction is not essential for society's definition of marriage, and if we consider the marriages of infertile couples to be valid, why not acknowledge loving and caring relationships of same-sex couples? These couples are incapable of the correct "type of sexual act that results in natural reproduction," says Sprigg in the same article. An infertile heterosexual couple can still be married because the right sexual pairing (of one man and one woman) is present in this relationship, which enables them to engage in the right type of sex. In other words the essence of marriage consists in the presence of the right pairing of genitals (i.e., the presence of a penis and a vagina).

Although it seems as if the importance of biological reproduction grounds this focus on heterosexual complementarity, other texts in Focus on the Family's universe deemphasize this importance of fertile sex. *Brio*, Focus's publication for teenage girls, tells its readers that, despite what they may hear around them, they intuitively know that marriage is a special and holy union between a man and a woman. As such it is not only a private matter but one that has important social tasks to fulfill: Marriage helps to order sexual relationships, and it unites in mutuality the "two parts of humanity" and "delivers mothers and fathers to children."[3] In *Breakaway*, the magazine for Christian teen boys, we read again the argument that marriage is not simply about private emotions and love. Rather, it is a public institution for a public benefit. Because every family needs a man and a woman, marriage is the tool to "bring them together."[4] Procreation is curiously absent in these arguments. The authors of the *Brio* article use the odd formulation that marriage "delivers" fathers and mothers to children. And the Bible verses quoted in *Breakaway* do not mention procreation but focus again on gender complementarity. We read about Genesis 1:26–27, the verse stating that God created man and woman to reflect his image, or about Genesis 2:18–24, saying that God created the woman because it was not good for man to be alone. And we learn that sex is divinely approved only if it happens between a husband and his wife.[5] By not including verse 28 in its quotation from Genesis (1:26–27), the *Breakaway* text stops short of making fertility part of the essential features of heterosexual marriage. The omitted verse 28 reads, "God blessed them and said to them, 'Be fruitful and increase in number; fill the earth and subdue it.'" Procreation is not a defining feature of a Christian marriage, but the presence of the right kind of sex organs or sexual complementarity is.

The importance of sexual complementarity is also reflected in the talking points that Focus makes available for town hall meetings and the like. Here is how, under the heading "Marriage in Jeopardy: Part 2," columnist Glenn Stanton describes the consequences of allowing same-sex couples to marry: Our ideas of marriage, parenthood, and gender will become meaningless, defined only by emotions, without resting on substantial differences.[6] Children will be taught a "'Mister Potato Head theory' of gender difference (same core, just interchangeable body parts)." Consequently, our notions of husband and wife or father and mother, or any concepts relating to gender differences, would become meaningless. This is the most threatening outcome of allowing same-sex couples to marry. Given that, according to Focus's text, society is held together by the union of the sexes, we see that the very bonds that unite the nation are at stake.

Because they lack the one essential feature of marriage, namely gender complementarity, allowing same-sex couples to marry would undermine this very institution. For example, Sprigg thinks that without legal recognition gays and lesbians who are currently married to heterosexual partners will have an incentive to stay in their current unions.[7] But more importantly, allowing same-sex couples to marry would lead to a change in how people conceive of marriage and in how they behave. These changes would be harmful to society because they would undermine the institution of marriage, which is a God-given gift and essential for the maintenance of a civilized nation, as we can read in *Breakaway*. Changing the contours of this divinely ordained institution would be "arrogant" and amounting to the claim that "we can improve on His creation."[8]

Moreover, gays and lesbians will bring their deviant and dangerous sexuality into the center of the American family, according to Sprigg. He states that "homosexual behavior is directly associated with higher rates of promiscuity, physical disease, mental illness, substance abuse, child sexual abuse, and domestic violence." The state cannot have any interest in rewarding this destructive conduct "by granting it society's ultimate affirmation—the status of civil marriage—or any of the benefits of marriage."[9] According to this argument, society affirms and rewards desired sexual and health-related behavior through admission to the coveted status of marriage. Moreover, admitting same-sex couples to the desired status of marriage will dissolve this very institution because homosexuals believe in indiscriminate and immediate sexual gratification and do not value commitment and fidelity, says Sprigg.

Because the gay and lesbian movement endorses sexual licentiousness, all gays and lesbians believe "that anybody should be able to have sex with anybody they want any time they want."[10] The sexual chaos that, according to Sprigg, is characteristic of what all gays and lesbians desire will spread through the entire nation.

Since we will encounter similar rhetorical moves elsewhere, let me point out the strategy of creating a single class of gays and lesbians whose political and sexual desires are defined by a unified cultural movement. This strategy not only prevents us from seeing the choices and ideals of individual men and women who live in same-sex partnerships, it also oversimplifies the story of the various sexual liberation movements in the United States. A call for sexual choice certainly was part of the cultural upheavals of the sexual revolution. Yet it is also noteworthy that, for example, the feminist anti-pornography movement of the late 1970s and early 1980s was organized by women who had spearheaded women's liberation. Given Focus's fear of a "Mr. Potato-Head" theory of gender, it is noteworthy that the anti-pornography feminists, including preeminent authors such as Mary Daley and Andrea Dworkin, believed in the *immutability* of sexual difference. Indeed, feminist Alice Echols comments critically that the anti-pornography movements "define male and female sexuality as though they were polar opposites. Male sexuality is driven, irresponsible, genitally oriented, and potentially lethal. Female sexuality is muted, diffuse, and interpersonally oriented."[11] This point is interesting because we will encounter in the texts of Focus on Family a very similar depiction of immutable male sexuality: an image of the violent man whose sexual aggression is somehow biologically given and who needs to be kept in check by the woman. Instead of a single unified movement that determines what their followers think, the story of feminism and gay and lesbian liberation is complex. It even provides us with an understanding of essential gender differences that many conservative Christians can echo.

For now, however, it is important to note that the texts of Focus are very invested in the idea that marriage is defined by sexual difference (the presence of the right combination of genitals). This difference is so central to

65

society's well-being that the state has a legitimate interest in preserving it and warding off any threat of dissolving this difference. For organizations such as Focus, changes in the sexual makeup of what they consider to be the essence of a natural and Christian marriage are therefore deeply threatening to the health of the nation. Marriage for gays and lesbians threatens nothing short of the dissolution of the state. Antisocial and dangerous behaviors will become socially acceptable, and the bonds that hold society together will unravel. This fearful language is echoed in the congressional debates about the so-called Defense of Marriage Act of 1996. One of the sponsors of the bill, Representative David Weldon from Florida, states his support for the act as follows:

> We must work to strengthen the American family, which is the bedrock of our society. And, marriage of a man and woman is the foundation of the family. The marriage relationship provides children with the best environment in which to grow and learn. We need to work to restore marriage, and it is vital that we protect marriage against attempts to redefine it in a way that causes the family to lose its special meaning. In the 1885 case of *Murphy v. Ramsey*, the U.S. Supreme Court defined marriage as the "union for life of one man and one woman in the holy estate of matrimony."[12]

In the Senate, Robert Byrd supported the act with a wide-ranging speech about marriage in the "Judeo-Christian" tradition, during which he quoted from his family Bible:

> I hold in my hands a Bible, the Bible that was in my home when I was a child. This is the Bible that was read to me by my foster father. It is a Bible, the cover of which, having been torn and worn, has been replaced. But this is the Bible, the King James Bible. And here is what it says in the first chapter of Genesis, 27th and 28th verses: "So God created man in his own image, in the image of God created he him; male and female created he them."[13]

A day earlier Senator Jesse Helms had declared that "homosexual extremists" attempted to attack the "nation's moral stamina" with the push for gay marriage, concluding that "at the heart of this debate is the moral and spiritual survival of this nation."[14]

These evocations of an unchangeable tradition and the anxious declarations together with their explicit theological underpinnings need explanation. How do we understand the claim that social stability is based on the bond between the "two parts of humanity," men and women? What is the characteristic of a spiritually uplifting Christian marriage that serves as a tonic to America's moral stamina? We thus need an analysis of the bonds that unite us and of the role sexuality (in marriage) and religion play in and for society. Examining marriage as the place where political, sexual, and religious concerns interact will help us understand why the debate about the love of same-sex couples is so intensely problematic for conservative Christians. And we will learn how their concerns echo in the wider American public.

To this end I will proceed in three steps: First, I will discuss the claim that there exists a single historical model of Christian marriage. Second, I will examine the contours of traditional American marriage and its connection to Christian values. Third, I will analyze from the perspective of political theory the idea that marriage and appropriate gender differences underlie a stable nation. Through these steps I argue that the conservative Christian claims in the current debates about marriage and same-sex unions have deep resonances in the self-understanding of the American polity. We will see how the gender arrangements of "traditional" marriage reflect the political needs of the modern nation-state. In particular, ideals of respectable masculinity and femininity are at stake. Thus, later in this chapter we will explore how respectable Christian sexuality is intertwined with concerns for the formation and preservation of the American middle class and its political interests.

67

THEOLOGIES OF CHRISTIAN MARRIAGE

In *Blessing Same-Sex Unions*, Mark Jordan presents us with a theological analysis of the various meanings of Christian marriage. Far from finding a unified or clear doctrine of the relationship between erotic love and Christian revelation, Jordan discloses that the center of the debates about "traditional marriage" is empty. The question of what is the essence of Christian marriage has no clear answers. Instead of a single Christian marriage tradition, Jordan finds a history of conflict.

What you will find in the history of theology (itself a narrative construct) is a long series of disagreements, some violent enough to split churches. Earlier still there is the awkward struggle to steady Christian ideals of sexual asceticism atop the evolving notions of marriage in Israel. No single marriage theology has held sway in all Christian churches, not least because of Christianity's deep ambivalences about sex and about Israel—which were, in the theological imagination, often enough combined.[15]

The requirements and conventions of marriage have changed numerous times in history. Who may marry whom, whether marriage is a Christian affair or not at all religious, and how consent is given—all this was open to debate and changing regulation. Jordan describes with great acuity the endless conflicts provoked by the questions of whether marriage is a Christian calling, whether it should be subject to church regulation, whether it can be dissolved, and what role (if any) procreation should play. For example, Paul notes in 1 Corinthians 7 that marriage is a (lamentable) remedy for human lustfulness, but he does not mention the need to procreate. What characterized Christian marriage was (and is) a matter of constant dispute among Christians. Instead of continuity we find a tumultuous history of innovations: Early Christians rejected pre-rabbinic Jewish marriage theologies, and reformed theologians denounced the idealization of chastity, which governed more than a thousand years of official church teaching on sexuality and marriage.

Jordan reminds us that early Christian sources, the New Testament among them, exhibited a clear ambivalence about the institution of marriage. As an institution wedded to the present (and decaying) order of the world, marriage does not help us enter into the new creation of the Kingdom of God that Jesus proclaimed. "For in the resurrection they neither marry nor are married, but are like angels in heaven" (Matthew 22:30). If marriage was debated by early theologians, the question was mostly whether the gospel prohibits marriage or whether it could be accepted as an inferior choice for Christians who could not contain their lustful desires. Virginity and chastity were the idealized Christian vocation, a point that Roman Catholic teaching upheld up to the second Vatican Council in the 1960s. Indeed, this scriptural skepticism about marriage is clear to one reader of *Brio* magazine who expresses confusion over Paul's counsel in 1 Corinthians

7:1 that Christians should not marry. *Brio*'s advice columnist, Susi Shellenberger, admits that the gift of "singleness," as she calls it, can help a person to lead a more God-centered life. Yet not everyone has this gift, and so God "brings men and women together" as teams so that they can minister better. (Note again the odd language of "bringing men and women together.")[16]

From the beginning of Christian thoughts about marriage, the onus seems to be on those finding reasons why this lifestyle can be spiritually productive, according to Jordan. Thus it is not surprising that in his exceedingly influential work *On the Marital Good*, Augustine aims to change the prevailing doctrine of marriage by arguing that it is not sinful for Christians to wed. Although he repeats that celibacy is the ideal Christian way of life, Augustine allows Christians to enter the bond of marriage if they need to gratify their sexual desires. It is better not to do so, but if they have to be sexually active, their intercourse can be morally acceptable only if it leads to procreation. Reproduction is therefore not the goal of marriage; rather, it is a remedy for making an otherwise sinful act (sexual intercourse) morally acceptable. Because not every sex act may lead to procreation, the married couple is always in danger of committing a sin. In this context, sexual abstinence and not fertility is the ideal. For Augustine procreation is itself problematic because it is linked to the unredeemed order of nature before Christ. The Kingdom will come not because Christians were fruitful and multiplied and thus kept the current world order alive but because of divine agency alone. Sexual abstinence is the right attitude toward the coming of the new world.[17]

At the same time, as Jordan reminds us, Augustine has to account for the precedent of polygamous marriages in the Old Testament. To the degree that they considered the Hebrew Bible to be part of the authentic revelation of God's plan, Christian theologians had to confront a disturbing fact: Abraham, Jacob, Moses, and many others had multiple wives. How could these patriarchs of old be considered holy men if they engaged not only in marriage but in polygamous ones? The stock answer of early Christian theologians such as Tertullian, Jerome, and Augustine was to claim that these ancient times required different measures and that we cannot know how chaste a life the patriarchs really lived. Yet in principle Augustine states that having multiple wives is not against the nature of marriage. Indeed, if reproduction is the natural goal of marriage, then we should expect Christian theologians to endorse polygamy, which maximizes the potential for offspring. This is the reason Thomas Aquinas used to justify a number of centuries later the polygamous practices of the patriarchs. For Augustine, the difference between patriarchal and Christian marriage is clear: "He distinguishes natural arrangements under the urgency of procreation from evangelical arrangements under the eschatological ideal of spiritual companionship. On this logic, a marriage theology that stresses nature and unlimited fertility is a theology for the patriarchs, not for Christians. Many contemporary 'Christian marriage theologies' would be, for Augustine, precisely non-Christian in their emphases."[18]

Nearly a millennium later, the European Reformation overturned the dominant theological precedent by critiquing the Augustinian idealization of celibacy. And although Luther rejects polygamy in principle, he endorses it at least in one case, as Jordan's research makes clear. One of Luther's powerful allies, Philip of Hesse, confided that he wanted to marry his concubine without giving up the marriage to his first wife, for fear of scandal. He had not been able to have sex with his wife, "for reasons of aversion," yet he could not live without sexual intercourse. Although he first resorted to a concubine, the duke later wanted to legitimize this relationship. Using the polygamous patriarchs as precedents, Luther and Melanchton secretly allowed Philip to engage in this second marriage. And Jordan comments, "You may want to regard the exception as Luther's throwing whatever scriptural rag he could find over an embarrassing incident. The remarkable thing is that he could conceive the second, bigamous marriage as valid without dissolving the first. To admit the validity of bigamous Christian marriage in even a single case opens the possibility of multiple simultaneous marriages."[19]

Christian theology's polyamory problem stems not only from the historical precedent of patriarchal polygamy. Jordan ingeniously shows that on the other end of the timeline, as it were, we find the expectation of an eschatological feast of universal love. Sixteenth-century Anabaptists and other restless Christian reform communities celebrated so-called Spirit-led marriages. Under the influence of the Holy Spirit men and women left their spouses and formed new erotic relationships. Because they rejected the earthly authority of church and state to regulate their marriages, these Anabaptists became branded as adulterers and polygamists. "For the Anabaptists themselves the 'Spirit-Marriages' seem to have been a sincere and often arduous attempt to place every act of sexual intercourse under the direct inspiration of the divine voice."[20] Although for some of us this project may seem to be as alien as early Christian idealizations of chastity, we find here a predecessor of the idea that God somehow destines us to find the right sexual partner. Yet not only individual fulfillment is at stake but a social vision according to which sexual desire overcomes social stratifications and binds us into a new communion of love. As such, Jordan argues, the Anabaptist movement was inspired by the Eucharistic feast as the anticipation of the fulfillment of time. Joining bodies together, regardless of sex and ethnic background, is the promise of the eschatological feast. Jordan concludes, "Christian theologians would think more clearly if they would admit that they have a polyamory problem not just with the patriarchs, but with the Eucharistic table and the Spirit that has been poured out into their hearts (Rom: 5:5)."[21] As we will see later, in the history of American romance the ideal of free sexual choice was indeed imagined as an expression of the Spirit's ability to bring us together in a communion of love.

In sum, instead of a timeless consensus about what constitutes Christian marriage we find Christians engaged in trying to make sense of the complexities of their scripture, desires, and histories. Instead of lamenting this absence of cohesion, Jordan cautions,

> My idealized marriage theology would prevent persons from settling too quickly on any account of their own lives, especially on accounts taken from campaign shouting, church chatter, or the sibilant seductions of the marketplace. It would do this by recalling as often as necessary how difficult it is to tell what divine agency might look like in erotically coupled lives.[22]

Before we continue by asking what stabilizes the meaning of marriage for conservative Christians and other Americans, let us consider the issue of divine agency. We have encountered the question of how to account for the action of the Spirit when Christians are reading scripture, and we learned about the need of the preacher and others to submit to its agency. In addition, we saw glimpses of how issues of divine power and of husbandly or fatherly authority interacted in conservative Christian ideals of marriage. In chapters 4 and 5 I will argue that Focus's language about male homosexuality reflects, oddly enough, an awareness of how difficult it is to describe the contours of divine agency in our lives. In other words, an embodied theology of grace is embedded in how Focus talks about same-sex love.

Jordan's theological analysis leaves us with this question: What is the centerpiece of the debates about marriage? What do we discuss when we talk about traditional marriage and the like?

> Discussions about marriage or mating are [today] controlled . . . by the endless cycling of mass images of romance. The images appear in many predictable places, from wedding homilies to "date" movies. They also figure where one might not expect them—say advertisements for gentrifying condos or TV spots for erectile dysfunction. It is remarkable how regularly the old romantic plots write themselves out in contemporary stories of desire, queer or not. . . . True desire becomes true love, or true love was true desire. Either redeems.[23]

72

According to Jordan, this romantic ideal of true love is marked by the marriage industry. Event planners, florists, caterers, photographers, and video artists (among others)—these are the specialists responsible for staging the great American wedding. In 2002, this wedding industry had a total revenue of $50 billion, and the average celebration came with a price tag of $20,000, writes Jordan. His analysis shows that not a single theology but the production and promise of the American wedding define Christian marriage for gays and lesbians (who desire it) and various Christians (who claim to defend it). Magazines such as *Modern Bride* and a host of industry specialists define the ritual appropriateness and lived theology of American Christian marriage. In this kind of marriage inherited theological tropes and Christian visions of erotic union are "reduced to chatter in thoughtless wedding sermons or in entertainment news about the latest Hollywood passion."[24] This chatter echoes even in Christian talk radio shows or "true Catholic" guide books for happy domesticity. They do not provide Christian countercultural imaginations but rather recycled versions of the ordinary theology of the American wedding, as Jordan claims.

In short, the debates about the great American wedding turn on mass-marketed images of romance. "In Christian churches and (other) queer cultures, discussions about marriage or mating are controlled not only by enforced institutional silences . . . but also by the endless cycling of mass images of romance."[25] These images reinscribe the narrative of seeking and (if all goes well) finding fulfillment on the body of the romantic lover. Jordan concludes, it therefore is a fallacy to think that there is one single thing (Christian marriage) that is now asked to embrace another single thing (love of same-sex partners). Instead we are confronted with an incessant chatter drowning out what Christianity could say about erotic love and preventing gays and lesbians from finding the words that could express their loves.

Jordan's theological analysis is another reminder that popular theologies are at stake in our debates, and not the preservation of historically anchored doctrines. At the same time, his work (including the quest for a true Christian theology of erotic love beyond the chatter of popular culture) underestimates the political context in which popular theologizing happens. However, political motives are important in how conservative Christians talk about the sanctity of marriage, as we have already seen. In his "Family Guides" Dobson tirelessly describes the threat that marriage for gay and lesbian couples poses to civilization. All values would be undermined and the world's children would be at risk—and, as a warning to America, Dobson states that all cultures that have allowed the collapse of the family quickly disintegrated.[26] For conservative Christian groups such as Focus, at least, talk about marriage is embedded not only in a web of romantic ideals but also in language about national stability. I will argue in the following section that this political concern for national stability and identity is one of the key factors that stabilize the ideal of romance and American Christian marriage theology. What conservative Christian organizations imagine as the traditional Christian marriage theology is formed in concert with these political concerns. To see this interaction, let me now trace the ménage à trois of sexuality, religion, and politics by recalling some historical debates about the character of the American marriage. Historicizing the ideal of romance, which Jordan showed to be central for the contemporary theological imagination, will allow us to see more clearly the role of religious speech in our polity.

AMERICAN (CHRISTIAN) MARRIAGE: A HISTORY OF CHANGE

American historian Nancy Cott shows very convincingly that debates about marriage law in the United States are connected to larger concerns about the contours and character of the American polity.[27] In debating marriage laws, Americans always debated the identity of their nation as well. An acceptable marriage, which can help to build society, was one that conformed to the ideal of romantic love. This ideal was importantly linked to the character of America as a Christian nation of European stock. For example, declaring as inadmissible aliens the spouses of marriages by proxy or polygamous relationships had the effect of restricting the number of Asian immigrants. Moreover, the monogamous marriages were meant to embody the standards of America as a *Christian* nation. U.S. officials were quick to believe that immigrants from groups they considered to be racially inferior (such as Jews and Asians) were incapable of forming the "true" romantic bonds that were the hallmarks of Christian marriage.

Cott points out that this twentieth-century connection between racial, religious, and national motives in immigration and marriage laws echoes the conflicts about polygamy that roiled the country in the previous century. In *Reynolds v. the United States*, the decision quoted by Congressman Weldon, the court declared that polygamy, which was practiced both by Mormons and by some Native American cultures, was a criminal act. Chief Justice Morrison Waite argued that considering polygamy as constitutionally protected under the First Amendment would "make religion 'superior to the law of the land' and every citizen 'in effect . . . a law unto himself.' "[28]

Does Waite's position imply that the state's interests are superior to the exercise of religion? Not quite. At the same moment when political interests seem to trump those of religion, we also see a connection between these two spheres through talk about America as a "civilized" nation. As we will see, the idea of American civilization is deeply connected to that of America as a Christian nation.

Like members of Congress who described Mormon women as "squaws" or "Mohammedans," Waite has an interpretation of polygamy that fuses religious and racist language in his discussion of American civilization. This marriage practice characterizes the peoples of Asia and Africa, and it

74

is alien, so believes the American judge, to the northern or western Europeans. At this point Waite echoes the opinions of the immensely influential forefather of American political science, German immigrant Francis Lieber, who writes,

> Monogamy does not only go with the Western Caucasian race, the Europeans and their descendants, beyond Christianity, it goes beyond Common Law. It is one of the primordial elements out of which all law proceeds, or which the law steps in to recognize and to protect. Wedlock . . . stands in this respect on a level with property. Wedlock, or monogamic marriage, is one of the "categories" of our social thoughts and conceptions, and therefore, of our social existence. It is one of the elementary distinctions—historical and actual—between European and Asiatic humanity. . . . It is one of the pre-existing conditions of our existence as civilized white men.[29]

On one hand, Lieber naturalizes monogamy as an original law- and society-producing institution, which has even deeper roots than the Common Law. Yet despite these echoes of the natural law tradition, he also characterizes monogamy as the hallmark of the civilizing achievements of the "white men," in contrast to what Lieber considers "Asian humanity." Europeans, Lieber's argument implies, are more civilized because they are closer to the primordial elements of natural law. They are both more cultured and more in tune with nature.

Lieber does not stand alone in his racial theory of civilization. For example, the marriages and gender relationships of the so-called uncivilized peoples are a favorite topic of talks given by female missionaries visiting the homeland. In these presentations and in numerous pamphlets the "primitive" woman appears as an uneducated, socially oppressed victim of total male dominance and sexual lust. This savage femininity is then contrasted with the status of the woman in the United States who enjoys the fruits of a Christian civilization. For the mainly female audience, who financed a substantial portion of the American mission effort, the message was made clear. "Christianity was portrayed as emancipatory . . . and the high position women enjoyed as the hallmark of Christian civilization in the United States."[30]

Another Supreme Court decision exhibits clearly the logic of connecting Christianity as the foundation of the American nation with talk about protecting women. In *The Mormon Church v. the United States of America* from 1890, Judge Joseph Bradley writes for the court that

> The organization of a community for the spread and practice of polygamy is, in a measure, a return to barbarism. It is contrary to the spirit of Christianity, and of the civilization which Christianity has produced in the western world.

The foundation of Bradley's argument is the claim that polygamy as a barbarian practice stands in contrast to Christianity's civilizing work in the west. He then asks rhetorically whether the political authorities had the right to sanction uncivilized practices if this meant hurting the interests of a truly civilized society. Through this question, Bradley shows what he considers to be a central task of American government action: protecting the interests of America as a civilized nation, that is, as a Christian nation. Nancy Cott concludes,

> The post–Civil War federal actions in favor of standard monogamy exerted a force for moral regulation. Implementing the views of the majority, they shaped individuals' beliefs and outlooks. Public policy that claimed to align itself with Christian civilization could be doubly efficacious in setting normative bounds. A refurbished alliance between national authority and Christian monogamous morality settled in place, prepared to badger nonconforming citizens if not to make them disappear—and to weed out marital nonconformists among the foreigners thronging the gates.[31]

Therefore, at the end of the nineteenth century we can see the following circle of arguments: (1) America as a civilized democracy insists that political interests trump what are considered "barbarian" religious practices, as Morrison Waite's 1878 decision in *Reynolds v. United States* made clear.[32] (2) America is part of the group of Christian cultures, and its government institutions are tasked with protecting its civilized status and the true interests of a cultured society, as we learned from Bradley's 1890 decision. Moreover, religious practices can enjoy constitutional protection only if they do not undermine America's character as civilized nation. Yet importantly, this civilized character itself is protected and supported by sexual institutions such as monogamous marriage, which are in turn religiously based. This means (3) that America's character as a democratic and civilized nation depends on European Christian sexual practices. And (4) the political authorities are tasked with protecting and supporting such religious practices.

From this short historical overview we can conclude that religions and political languages interact in the debates about correct sexual practices. Let us now analyze this connection from the perspective of political theory.

PROTECTING THE BODY POLITIC: A POLITICAL ANALYSIS

To begin let me recall two points: First, protection of the civilized character of America stands at the center of the debates about and legislative actions surrounding marriage and polygamy. Second, this care for the American body politic is connected to civilizing practices that regulate individual sexuality and aims to produce good citizens.

Part of this civilizing work happens through the institution of marriage, which shapes both the private and the political. Let me highlight two points: First, the institution of marriage exhibits clearly the connections between the state's care for itself (its identity, boundaries, and character) and the shaping of acceptable individual sexuality. Second, given the importance of these connections, it is to be expected that concerns about the institution of marriage are particularly poignant in situations where the identity of the body politic is perceived to be threatened. As we can learn from the history of European colonialism, these are the phases of foreign dominance when overtly violent subjugation of the native population morphs into their bureaucratic incorporation into an allegedly common polity.[33] At this point several questions arise: What is the legal status of the colonized people in contrast to a native of, say, England or Germany? What rights do women have who marry a nonnative husband? What is the racial and legal status of children who were born to European mothers and indigenous fathers? Similar questions appeared in times of mass immigration in the United States. In 1907, for example, Congress declared that "any American woman who marries a foreigner shall take the nationality of her husband," a view that Ethel MacKenzie, who was married to a Briton, challenged in 1911. In that year, women had received the right to vote in the State of California. Rejecting her claim, the U.S. Supreme Court invoked what the justices considered the "ancient principle [of] the identity of husband and wife," under male dominance, as Cott reports. Consequently, women who married foreigners lost their U.S. citizenship, and American men who married foreign-born women conferred U.S. citizenship to them and to their future children. Cott describes an attempt to reduce the number of Chinese immigrants as the racial context in which this legal arrangement was considered plausible. It was not Ethel MacKenzie's English husband who represented the face of the feared diluting of the American body politic but the potential that a so-called white American woman could be under the legal submission of an Asian American husband. Cott reminds us that at the time eight states had laws against "whites" marrying Japanese or Chinese and she concludes, "If marriages produced the polity, then wrongfully joining marriages could be fatal." In short, marriage is not a private affair but essential for the maintenance of the correct boundaries of the body politic.[34]

78

These historical considerations provoke the systematic questions of the reason for this political importance of marriage, the role of religion in it, and how it relates to the ideal of romance that Jordan described.

Hand in hand with marriage's function to build the body politic goes the ideal of marriage as based on free assent, which is a fundamental idea in American political theory. Following Montesquieu, Christian monogamous marriage is linked to the ideal of the free republic. "As a voluntary union based on consent, marriage paralleled the new government. This thinking propelled the analogy between the two forms of consensual union in the republican nation's self-understanding and identity."[35] This ideal of free union was contrasted with British colonial rhetoric likening the relationship between crown and subject to that between the father and his household.

Thus, it is not surprising that we find during the struggle for American independence a host of pamphlets praising the state of marriage, which is seen as the emblem of free attraction and mutuality of interest. As Cott informs us, John Witherspoon argued that marriage is the highest case of human friendship and requires equality in education, taste, and conduct of life. The ideal of the romantic bond of marriage that is based on free assent became popularized over the years, so much so that it was experienced as a particularly American institution. For example, memoirs of European immigrants often point to the harsh and oppressing marriage customs in their home countries and how America allowed them to form romantic bonds according to their own choosing. The sentiment that marriage based on free attraction is a quintessential American institution also appears in Robert and Helen Lynd's study *Middletown*. Summarizing their findings about life in the typical American town between 1890 and 1925 they write, "The townsfolk seemed to regard romance in marriage as something which, like their religion, must be believed in to hold society together."[36] Romance and religion are essential for the perfect unity in marriage and in society.

ROMANCE AND BICKERING

The ideal of the modern republic and that of the modern romantic institution of marriage are built around a free flow of communication, which is unhindered by the boundaries of social class. Jane Austen's talkative Emma seems so contemporary to us because like her we are incensed when the immensely rich and powerful Lady DeBurgh claims that Emma has not enough social standing to even be speaking to her. As far as the ideal romance or ideal republic is concerned, everyone can have social intercourse with everybody else.

American philosopher Stanley Cavell makes a similar point in his work on Hollywood movies, which he uses to develop his own brand of political theory. Because the marriage bond is seen as so essential in the formation of the American body politic, Cavell analyzes what keeps the couple together, what binds them in perfect unity, and what characterizes this unity. Cavell engages this set of questions with an interest in reunion. This focus on forming again the marital and political union makes sense, given the numerous disruptions of the political union in the United States and the memories of the most radical of those, the Civil War. Thus, Cavell understands the screwball comedies of the 1930s and 1940s to be "comedies of remarriage." A movie of this genre has the following characteristic: "The drive of its plot is not to get the central pair together, but to get them *back* together, together *again*. . . . Something evidently internal to the task of marriage causes trouble in paradise—as if marriage, which was to be a ratification, is itself in need of ratification."[37] The question these films raise is not what an ideal marriage bond *looks* like but how it *sounds*. Cavell's answer is (appropriately) "constant bickering." Not the cessation of dissonance but the ability to maintain a state of perpetual verbal exchange characterizes the ideal marital—and by extension political—union. Marriage is not a static institution but a continuous performance of verbal exchanges. Through these exchanges we form and maintain the bonds of affection (and dissonance) that characterize loyalty to home and state. Thus, the perfect state of union must be continuously spoken into being.

This idea of marriage and society as speech act is a critique of social contract theories of the modern liberal states, from Rousseau to Rawls. Before we can even enter into a contract, the question arises whether we are willing to listen and speak to each other. The thesis that the bonds of society are contractual in nature overlooks the fact that I have to see the other as partner *before* entering the contractual obligation. As the history of Native Americans in the United States shows, contracts are only as good as the underlying respect of the parties involved. The conception of society as the set of individuals who are bonded to each other by contract-like obligations (or trade-offs of interests, as we might say) presupposes the existence of a community of basic mutual respect. According to Cavell, the marriage contract (as well as the ideal of the social contact) requires that we be willing to shape this underlying community by speaking together (i.e., through intercourse in language). Through his focus on marriage, Cavell locates this struggle for a shared language in the space of sexual intimacy. This move highlights the importance of something allegedly private (sexual desire) in the creation of the political bond.

Sexual desires, the drive to find fulfillment on, with, in, and through the body of another person, are formed through social interactions. This is a point that we find echoed in Focus on the Family literature. As I mentioned in chapter 1, Focus's ministry is shaped by the profound incorporation of modern therapeutic ideals into the theology of conservative Christianity. Developmental psychologist Joseph Nicolosi, who counts as an authority on therapeutic issues for Focus, states that "masculinity is an achievement." He insists that great care has to be taken so that children can form the right kind of gender identity, including the right kind of sexual desires.[38] In general, the importance of sexual discipline lies in the following: Who we are as sexually desiring beings depends on how we are disciplined by parents, peers, schools, churches, and other institutions of authority. These provide strictures through which we become socially viable subjects, citizens whose inner lives are shaped in line with social expectations.

In Cavell's view, sexuality is the place where the formations of our inner lives and that of our public subjectivity interconnect. Here the realm of the inner turns into the outer, and the demands of society help shape the inner space of subjectivity.[39] In disciplining sexual desires, society aims to produce subjects who are capable of forming the bonds of affection that are considered to foster the interests of the state. The desires of our inner lives are not simply our own; they are shaped by social forces and for society's interests. In sum, if romantic attraction and marriage out of free consent provide the founding metaphor of our modern polity, then it is important to shape sexual desire in the image of romantic fulfillment. Looking back at Jordan's observations about the ubiquity of the romantic narrative, we can conclude that it is held in place not simply through the power of the marriage industry but also for political reasons. The belief that love can strike at any point, and that we must be free to choose whom we want to marry, is central for the self-understanding of the American polity. Yet romance is only one part of the equation of what makes an appropriate marriage.

THE RESPECTABLE NATION

Historian George Mosse shows in his *Nationalism and Sexuality: Respectability and Abnormal Sexuality in Modern Europe* a similar connection between the formation of sexual identity and the political subject. According to him, the modern nation-state has two foundations: constitutional government and respectability.[40]

With respectability Mosse describes a regime of sexual and moral discipline aimed at shaping the desired middle-class subject. Virtuous masculinity, self-control, obedience, thrift, and a sense for duty and self-fulfillment through good work characterize the ideal bourgeois citizen. For the cases of Britain and Germany, Mosse shows how these virtues, which originate in eighteenth-century Protestantism, support a deluge of respectability in the early nineteenth century. Like that of romance novels, we find a flood of manuals of manners, such that within a generation there appears a shift to an extremely heightened awareness for propriety.

The regime of respectability allows the newly formed middle classes to present themselves as legitimate holders of political power. Codes of respectability force distance between the licentious world of the nobility and the uncivilized laborers. Through this strategy, the burgeoning middle class could present itself as embodiment of true civilization and true national values with a legitimate claim to take over the structures of government. As we have already seen in Cott's history of American marriage law, the idea of civilization evokes a complex set of Christian, colonial, and racist resonances. However, what is the connection between respectability and the other pillar of the modern nation-state, constitutional government?

The idea of constitutional government goes hand in hand with the vision that the people are the sovereign of the modern nation-state. The ideal citizen is both subject and sovereign. Thus, we can find an implicit two-body theory for the democratic nation-state. The "body corporeal" of the individual citizen embodies the character of the ideal body politic. Like the body of the king that was meant to represent the totality of the realm, the ideal citizen has to incorporate and display the contours of national identity. This democratization of the representative functions of the body of the sovereign means that the individual body has to be disciplined according the nation's ideals. It is not enough to show outward loyalty toward the body of the sovereign; the citizen has to become this body by behaving like a "true Englishman" or a "real American." At issue is not the right paperwork but cultural authenticity. (For example, Asian Americans who have lived in the United States for generations still report being asked, "Where are you *really* from?" The implication is that they must be foreign born, something that would not happen to someone, say, of Italian extraction.) Not only is the force of oppressive state powers democratized through the psychological mechanisms of internalization but so is the care for national "civilized" identity.

Because respectability is linked to gender-specific expectations about sexual behavior, we can see a sexual division of labor in the task of embodying the body politic. Women have to adhere to different standards of appropriateness than men. Yet the disciplining of both bodies aims to achieve respectable sexual relationships.

These expectations become clear in the context of the modern romantic marriage. First the barrage of romantic images and narratives helps shape the expectation that marriage embodies the citizen's freedom to form erotic and thus social bonds, independent of inherited class differences. They can form in freedom a new perfect union of equals. Second, the romantic marriage presupposes that the parties to this union enter and maintain respectable relationships. The codes of respectability ensure a new social and racial differentiation in favor of American white middle class. Romantic marriage is only supportive of the nation-state if it adheres to middle-class national values. The language of romance allows the overcoming of traditional social differentiations in the shaping of a new national community, yet standards of respectability introduce and successfully solidify new hierarchies in the interests of the politically decisive middle class.

Respectability appears in American political rhetoric from the moment that the new polity established itself. Cott mentions an Independence Day declaration from 1790 in which the preservation of virtue and manners was depicted as essential for the survival of the nation. "Dissipation and corruption of manners in the body of the people [is as much a danger] to the liberties and freedom of our country as was power-grabbing by rulers."[41] Women were tasked with upholding the manners of the newly formed Republic, which seems unsurprising given what we heard from Chatterjee in chapter 2. " 'In a republic manners are of equal importance with laws'; and while men made the laws, 'the women, in every free country, have an absolute control of manners.' " Even more explicit is John Adams, who declares in 1778 after a visit to the French Court, "The Jews, the Greeks, the Romans, the Swiss, the Dutch, all lost their public Spirit, their Republican Principles and habits, and their Republican form of government, when they lost the Modesty and Domestic Virtue of their Women." Accordingly, the state needs respectable marriages and, to this end, respectable women who acknowledge the husband's dominance and leadership. Women are called to joyfully submit to the husband's leadership. In 1793, one essayist wrote that in the union of marriage they abdicated some of their natural rights in return for male protection, as men abdicate some of their rights when they enter into the political union of the state. Consequently, writes this self-proclaimed friend of the "fair sex," rebellious behavior by women in marriage is as "odious" as "any other opposition to a just, mild and free political government." Having chosen freely their attachment, women now need to submit to the lawful authority of their husbands, who, having entered the free covenant of the republic, have to submit to political authority. The promise of freedom (and romance) goes only so far, and revolution has to give way to lawful government.[42]

Respectability and romance thus enter an unstable union in the modern marriage ideal. The weakening of premodern status hierarchies made possible the formation of the new middle-class citizen as a respectable and romantic subject. It is characterized therefore by two conflicting demands: the romantic overcoming of traditional class differences through free attachments and the need to maintain class and race hierarchies through respectability. Our analysis shows that the middle-class self has to permanently negotiate this instability. Such subjectivity is formed through the disciplining of sexual attractions, which are supposed to lead into an appropriate romantic marriage. Thus, these negotiations aim at forming appropriate desires and attachments in respectable and romantic selves.[43]

84

CONCLUSION: RELIGION, RESPECTABILITY, AND THE GREAT AMERICAN WEDDING

From this historical and political analysis we can learn why issues of marriage are so politically charged and how religious narratives about sexuality are part of the American ideal of romance and respectability. Mark Jordan is right to claim that not a single coherent Christian tradition but the script of romance stabilizes what we can call the American public theology of marriage. Yet we should make the following additions. This script of romance operates together with the script of respectability, and both are held in place by a political rationale: the self-definition of American middle-class identity and thus the (re)hierarchizing of the American polity. Romance creates the idea that all Americans form a society in perfect union, independent of their backgrounds, and respectability makes sure that this perfect union remains stratified with clear boundaries defining who is and is not part of the political process.

Respectability therefore provides a sorting dynamic that establishes power differences within the social order. Evelyn Brooks Higginbotham coined the concept of "politics of respectability" in her work on the women's movement in the black Baptist church in the late nineteenth and early twentieth century. She shows how black women used the ideal of respectability to resist racist images of the black woman as immoral and uncivilized, thus turning against racist oppression a tool that was deployed originally to legitimize African American disenfranchisement. Respectability, Higginbotham holds, was a mixture of middle-class ideals such as "temperance, industriousness, thrift, refined manners, and Victorian sexual mores." With its roots in churches, the politics of respectability allowed black women to claim being part of the perfect union of the American polity. The goal was to find "a common ground to live as Americans with Americans of other racial and ethnic backgrounds." In the context of our analysis, we might say it was an attempt to be part of the romantic imagination of America, according to which all Americans are bonded in perfect union. As such, it was an "attack on the failure of America to live up to its liberal ideals of equality and justice and an attack on the values and lifestyle of those blacks who transgressed white middle-class propriety."[44] Higginbotham's work shows how the appeal to the romantic idea that all Americans form one united society can be made only on the basis of dominant white respectability. Romance thus begets exclusion and internal stratification.

How can we then assess the discussions about opening marriage to gays and lesbians and the persistent claim of conservative groups such as Focus on the Family that such unions undermine the fabric of society? According to our analysis we can see that these debates display the tensions between romance and respectability in the shaping of the American body politic.

The first important insight is that our individual bodies are not simply private. An intricate cooperation of social forces (using the intertwining of political and religious language) co-produces the space of the private, and with it acceptable intimate desires. What we do with our bodies, even in the intimate sphere of sexuality, is therefore inherently of public interest and in principle open for public control. This does not mean that there is no positive or constitutional right to privacy; rather, my claim is that what constitutes privacy and what we desire from intimacy are shaped by public interests and negotiations.

Conservative Christian organizations are therefore right to see a connection between how we organize our sexual relations and how we establish the

85

boundaries and character of our nation. In so doing they repeat a long-standing tradition in American political and legal theory, and they tap into deeply held popular beliefs about the character of the nation. Yet the connections they see are not given in the nature of sexuality or sociality; rather, they reflect the political needs of the modern democratic nation-state. Thus the question arises: Can one make an argument for admitting gays and lesbians to this tradition of modern respectable romance in the national interest?

ROMANCE AND FREE CHOICE

On one side of the debate about marriage for same-sex partners, we hear the argument that Americans have the fundamental right to choose one's life partner. As Alaskan judge Peter Michalski stated, "The relevant question is not whether same-sex marriage is so rooted in our traditions that it is a fundamental right but whether the freedom to choose one's life partner is so rooted in our tradition."[45] Judge Michalski here relies on the romantic ideal of freely chosen love. Given how central this ideal is to the formation of a middle-class subjectivity and citizenry, it is clear that the state has an interest to protect and foster this freedom of choice.

However, the argument assumes that same-sex desire shapes itself according to the American codes of romance. In order to enter the arena of legal rights (and public acknowledgment), gay and lesbian relationships have to talk about themselves in a specific narrative script. And according to Jordan, this is what happens increasingly:

> Identities for same-sex desires have been written by many regimes and their agents, including preachers, inquisitors, judges, and physicians. Today they get written increasingly by the purveyors of romance, those charming successors to the preachers, inquisitors, and physicians. They are . . . wedding preachers who want to preside over every coupling of "identical genitals." They do so not only by direct prescription, but by reinforcing romance in the imagined space of queer subculture.[46]

In the attempts to romanticize every instance of same-sex desire, a line is drawn to define what is and what is not appropriate. Only couplings that are embedded in truly romantic relationships count; neither the fleeting encounters between the massage therapist and the family man nor the ménage à trois involving partners of the same sex fulfills the script of romance. As in Evelyn Higginbotham's analysis of black politics of respectability, entrance into the realm of acceptable desire involves adhering to a set of middle-class norms. These are the norms that make sexual desire into an instance of respectable romance.

Let us recall that the script of true romance promises to the couple fulfillment in each other and holds out for them the hope of finding their destiny. Yet it requires also the presence of true desire, leading to true love and thus stable sexual identities. And importantly, this quest for sexual identity is itself framed in romantic terms. We have to voyage to discover our true nature through the perils of coming out or through the sequence of Christian conversion, conviction, and belief.

I do not wish to belittle the importance of this narrative; after all, our inner lives are shaped by it, and it would be close to impossible to discard it. Yet I question Cott's claim that the exalted status of coupled love in our society is simply a given and demands no explanation. It is true that "love is exalted in our society—it is the food and drink of our imagination. Sexual love has even more of a halo, because we assume that an individual's full subjectivity blossoms in the circle of its intimacy."[47] Yet these ideals are not simply there (as if given by nature). They are shaped by a multifaceted discourse in which language about our most intimate selves resonates in political and religious registers. The political pressure of forming a national identity binds together the many idioms—racial, medicinal, literary, legal, and theological—that create the modern language of love. The language of love in turn resonates over all these registers. It affects how we experience ourselves and how our subjectivity is formed.

As we learned from Cavell's reflections on psychoanalysis and political theory, our sexual desires are molded in such a way that we become romantic and thus politically viable subjects. Invoking the right to marry for romantic gay and lesbian couples implies conceiving of their experiences and their desires according to a narrative that essentially supports American nation building. (Some theorists of gay and lesbian liberation may reject the quest for marriage as a bourgeois endeavor. Yet Jordan shows how deeply engrained romantic images are even in the quest for a gay or lesbian counter culture. "Gay liberation . . . was an utopian fantasy . . . in which properly directed love would recreate the world."[48]) Becoming romantic subjects in turn implies the mobilization of religious language, independently of whether we consider ourselves religious. For example, Jordan shows the deep theological roots of the American language of romance.

> Consider some constitutive elements. In true love, you find the one right person and give yourself entirely to him, to her. . . . The total gift of yourself to the other completes you, makes you for the first time who you were really meant to be. . . . Your gift to each other creates a couple that can stand against the cruel, uncomprehending world of those who oppose your love. If the world doesn't understand, God will understand, because God made your love. . . . In cycling codes of romantic etiquette, true love not only relies on religious terms and notions, it ends by arrogating to itself the place of the divine.[49]

Romantic references to the freedom to choose a partner do not escape popular American theologies. Religiously infused language and images prevail and with them the interconnections of sexuality, the nation, and the divine.

RESPECTABILITY

Even if same-sex desire adheres to the code of romance, the question can be raised whether such romantic attachments are indeed respectable. After all, only respectable romance is fit to build society, according to the codes of the romantic nation-state. Whereas romance came with the promise of binding us all together, respectability involved the goal of making sure that this perfect union has a clear hierarchy. Softer than the coercive mechanisms of state institutions, this strategy aims to control the access to and the flow of power in the middle-class nation-state. In fact, reverting to overt government actions is evidence of the nation's failure to control behavior, desire, and thoughts. Miscegenation laws, or those banning extending the duties and benefits of marriage to gays and lesbians, are necessary only if the thought of an interracial couple or one consisting of partners of the same sex is possible. The regime of respectability works best if the undesired behavior appears to all parties concerned (those with social standing) to be naturally offensive, such that state intervention is only minimally necessary.

Disreputable love is by definition socially corrosive. One cannot build a society on indecent attachments. By declaring the love of same-sex couples to be seedy, offensive, scandalous, disrespectable, and so on, conservative Christian organizations evoke the register of disgust. Although a society may need to tolerate people of ill repute, they and their desires cannot be allowed at the center of our society. Hence, conservative Christian arguments against allowing marriage for gay and lesbian couples are full of language invoking the indecent nature of such relationships.

In *Marriage Under Fire: Why We Must Win This Battle*, Dobson states that it is a slippery slope from marriage for gays and lesbians to marriages "for daddies and their little girls or between a man and his donkey."[50] This association between romantic relationships of Americans of the same sex with incest or with sex between men and animals appears over and over again in the political forum. The former Republican U.S. Senator Rick Santorum famously likened sexual activity between same-sex couples to "man on dog" sex, and Democratic New York State assemblyman Dov Hinkind suggested that if the State of New York allowed same-sex couples to marry, then the assembly should also legalize incest. And Congressman James Talent argued that "if marriage goes, then the family goes, and if the family goes, we have none of the decency or ordered liberty which Americans have been brought up to enjoy and to appreciate."[51]

Dobson's slippery slope argument presupposes first that the meaning and scope of marriage are traditionally stable. After all, without an alleged stable starting point, we can have no decline on the slippery slope. Second, this argument claims that if we lose this assumed stability, than there is no rational way to distinguish between a woman who loves another woman on one hand and someone having sex with a dog on the other. It is clear that Dobson's texts assume both points. As for the first part of the argument, he writes that "the family as it has been known for more than five millennia will crumble, presaging the fall of Western civilization itself."[52] However, we have seen that Christian or American marriage is a very plastic institution, which has undergone many transformations during its existence. In other words, the meaning of marriage was always slippery. Apparently, this institution did evolve and change; particularly in the last 100 years we see a movement to include in its purview more and more people who were previously excluded from it.

Regarding the second argument, we learned that our public negotiations about who should be part of the American polity (and who shouldn't) kept in place how America understood marriage. Not one single definition ("marriage is the union of one man and one woman") but a host of plausibilities, romance and respectability among them, stabilizes the reach of this institution. Likewise, the romantic ideal that we can marry the lover of our choice is not an abstract right but part of a web of proprieties. In traditional American political theory, one rationale for the state's support of romantic marriages between consenting adult human beings was the following: The perfect union of the state requires romantic subjects, such that they are drawn to each other not because of familiarity or coercion but because they desire to enter their society in free consent. In so doing they are willing to overcome differences of social background. As long as we do not consider donkeys or dogs to be citizens, the state should have no interest in sanctioning unions with such or any other animals. It is therefore not true that we have no means to distinguish between the "man-on-man" and the "man-on-donkey" case. Surely for some of us there is a crucial difference between finding romantic fulfillment with another human being and claiming to do this on the body of an animal. The argument that marriage for gays and lesbians leads to marriages between a man and donkey works only if we are (or make ourselves) blind to this difference.

What does work, however, is the argument that if we open the door for one kind of smut, it is going to be difficult to keep other kinds out. In other words, Dobson's claims against marriage for gays and lesbians are convincing to the degree that we already are prepared to consider loving a person of the same sex to be as reprehensible as having sexual relations with a child or an animal. The prior conviction that such conduct is beyond the scope of respectability makes this argument work. The argument does not function by pointing out the disastrous consequences of this decision but by making clear that something is wrong with it from the beginning. If we think that nothing is morally wrong about same-sex love, then legalizing such marriages is unproblematic. Yet if we already think that the relationships of gays and lesbians are egregiously morally problematic, then sanctioning them through marriage would be as absurd as endorsing other equally reprehensible couplings. Instead of being the institution that fosters a respectable state, marriage would become a travesty.

In sum, Dobson's slippery slope argument is not really an argument; rather, it is a reiteration of a prior conviction: Erotic love between couples of the same sex is egregiously reprehensible, on a par with other horrid and sinful things, such as child abuse or sex with animals. In drawing a connection between the man who loves another man and one who has intercourse with a donkey, Dobson conjures up images of an outlandish sexuality. In so doing he aims at instilling a sense of the moral bankruptcy of a society that is willing to endorse marriage for people who are engaging in sexual acts as allegedly depraved as same-sex love. Thus, at stake is not whether we can distinguish between loving a human being and loving an animal; at stake is whether we consider erotic love between members of the same sex as something that could be considered "respectable." Republican congressman Charles Canady, one of the chief sponsors of the Defense of Marriage Act, expressed this point during the congressional debate of the bill: "What is really at stake [is] whether the law of this country should treat homosexual relationships as morally equivalent to heterosexual relationships. . . . Should this Congress tell the children of America that it is a matter of indifference whether they establish families with a partner of the different sex or cohabit with someone of the same sex?"[53]

After our short overview of the history of the American marriage it is not surprising that some legislators think it is the business of Congress to use marriage legislation to uphold the moral standards of the land. And it should be clear that the one stable characteristic of "traditional marriage" in America is this: Legislators have jealously guarded their prerogative to shape it according to their religious and political interests. "Where public authorities a century earlier had been primed to defend Christian-model monogamy from free love, interracial coupling, polygamy, self-divorce, and commercial sex, now Congress found heterosexuality the crucial boundary to maintain."[54]

HETEROSEXUAL STRATIFICATION

Why is heterosexuality the battle line on which to defend the ideal of the respectable American romance? Note that the overwhelming majority of those who consider same-sex love as sinful rank it on a level with adultery.

Only 7 percent of committed Evangelicals think that such love is a sin worse than adultery.[55] However, we see nowhere a coalition of Christian organizations championing, with broad public support, the outlawing of adultery, and there are no attempts to make divorce illegal or to ban infertile people from getting married. Yet neither the couple's fidelity nor their fertility is at stake, as we saw. The decisive issue is their heterosexuality, specifically their middle-class respectable heterosexuality.

I have argued that the regime of respectability allowed the creation of power differentials for the benefit of the middle class, and we saw that the discipline of romance was aimed at creating the right structure of desire, one that helped produce the nation-state. Thus the defense of heterosexuality does not aim primarily at disempowering a minority of homosexuals, as long as they follow the script of romantic love.[56] After all, why should Americans be so concerned about preventing a small minority of their fellow citizens from living their sexual lives? Same-sex couples represent such a small minority that the intense political battle about their marriage rights seems disproportionate. More must be at stake. And this is the complex of romance and respectability itself, one that aims at shaping the contours of normative middle-class heterosexuality.

Economic realities have changed the married couples' relations to each other. Middle-class women contribute substantially to their families' upkeep, and the one-income household is neither the rule in American suburbia nor a widely shared ideal. And as far as the state is concerned, mutual consent seems to be the only criterion to judge the morality of heterosexual relations.

> State legislators and courts have moderated their former definitional role and resuscitated their much earlier willingness to treat couples "living together" as if they were married, at least in economic terms. The families of unmarried couples are treated as families in court. Parents' rights over children do not diminish . . . just because of birth out of wedlock. This public willingness to see [heterosexual] marriage-like relationships as marriages is driven by the aim of guaranteeing economic support by family members . . . but it also diversifies social views of family relationships.[57]

What remains to be regulated is an appropriate understanding of the ideal heterosexual gender and sexual difference. The strategy of declaring same-sex desire to be outside the purview of respectable sexuality helps to maintain this ideal, and with it the implied power differences between men and women.

The ideal heterosexual difference regulates not only the flow of power within a family. Rather, this idea is connected to both political and theological considerations. As a Southern Baptist woman states to Gallagher, "I think there is a lack of respect for God because we've lost the idea of a husband's authority. They say you usually relate to God through the image your father presents of him. And if there is no father there, then how are you going to see what He is really like, and how are you going to look to God with respect and authority." In this woman's words, specific ideas about her husband's authority or that of her father and about the power of God are interconnected and can mutually illuminate each other. Gallagher comments that for Evangelical Christians this hierarchy of gender reflects an ordered reality reaching from their biological bodies, to all of creation, and finally to God.[58] Although Gallagher does not expand on these points, we will analyze over the course of the next two chapters how these theological ideas about power are embodied in the Christian sexual life and how they are intertwined with political needs.

Examining these relationships between sexual norms and politics is important, because the family is not only the place where American Christians learn about the right understanding of God and divine power. It is also the place where they learn about the nation, as we have seen in our discussions of Chatterjee, Mosse, and Cavell. The nation is perceived as a "male-headed household in which both men and women have 'natural' roles to play," as Joane Nagel summarizes the use of gender differences in nationalist movements.[59] In the next chapter I will analyze in detail how conservative Christian modes of talking about same-sex love contribute to the creation of normative Christian and American masculinity and femininity. I will explain why male homosexuality is a focal point for conservative Christian concerns about America. And we will discuss the concomitant ideal of female submission in the family.

In this chapter we have seen how religious concerns are part of the shaping of American national identity. And we have learned how central the institution of marriage was for this process, via the ideals of romantic love and respectable middle-class sexuality. Religious language is part of the patchwork of images and ideals that form the self-understanding of the American nation. The ideal and practice of the grand American wedding, which both Jordan and Cott see as characteristic for how we organize our sexual relations, is thus motivated by state interests and not only by the wedding industry. The language of romance and respectable love, which animates popular American theologies of sexuality, is kept in circulation through political and religious channels. This chapter demonstrated for the American context the public nature of religious values and languages. What counts as acceptable and as "traditional" Christian marriage theology develops in the context of political interests that are forming and supporting the modern nation-state. At the same time, these interests are shaped through language and images related to Christianity. Thus religious and political language are co-produced, and each reinforces the other.

SAME-SEX LOVE AND THE IMPOSSIBILITY
OF CHRISTIAN FEMININITY AND MASCULINITY

As we saw in chapter 3, conservative Christian organizations fear that allowing marriage for same-sex couples
would threaten the ideal heterosexual structure of society.
At stake is a specific understanding of what constitutes the
heterosexual difference. To understand why this is the case
and what characterizes this difference, we need to take a
closer look at how same-sex love appears in conservative
Christian texts. Therefore this chapter analyzes how Focus
on the Family depicts same-sex love and its threat to the
heterosexual order. We will see that male homosexuals are
talked about most frequently in Focus literature. In it, two
specific stereotypical images of gays are presented promi-
nently, which I call the oversexed hyper-male and a gender-
insecure hypo-male. I argue that these two images function
to delineate normative Christian masculinity as an unstable
composite of dominant aggression and submission. The
masculinized lesbian or the feminist operates in tandem
with these depictions of male homosexuality. Particularly
in discourses of proper female submission to male headship,

Focus's texts invoke the dangerous influence of feminism as confusing women about the value of proper biblical submission. Feminists and lesbians are portrayed as women who reject the right male authority over their lives. Yet what submission is supposed to mean remains unclear both in Focus's texts and in the lives of many ordinary Evangelicals. Instead of an unambiguous picture of Christian masculinity or femininity, the texts of Focus present us a normative Christian sexuality that is fraught with tensions and ambiguity. The rhetorical construction of gays, lesbians, and feminists allows delineation of normative masculinity and femininity; they are part of a strategy enabling a field of contestation for what it means to be a Christian man or woman. What then constitutes the heterosexual difference? Not stability but a drama of contestation over agency, aggression, power, and submission.

GAYS AND FEMINISTS: FROM LOGIC TO RHETORIC

96 To begin, I shall mention two methodological points. First, I will explain how these depictions of gays and feminists function as mirror images in conservative Christian texts about the family. Second, I will clarify why I shift in the following to what I call a rhetorical analysis of how Focus talks about male homosexuals.

Dobson's arguments against marriage for same-sex partners interweave three rhetorical threads, as we have seen: the value of the family, the divine order of the sexes, and the stability of nation and society. For example, following British social anthropologist Joseph Daniel Unwin (1895–1936), Dobson states that "the energy that holds a society together is sexual in nature." By this he means that a man who is devoted to "one woman and one family" will be motivated to be productive, innovative, and thrifty for the sake of his loved ones. "However, when male and female sexual interests are dispersed and generalized, their effort is invested in the gratification of sensual desires."[1] Dobson thinks the threat to American civilization arises from forces that, by destabilizing human gender identity, dissolve the sexual glue that unifies society and family. Dobson identifies two of these forces: homosexuality and feminism.

A closer look at the Focus Web sites reveals that the "homosexual agenda" is the prime threat in the perceived assault on the American family. We find homosexuality among the "hot topics" linked on Focus's main portal, but we do not find feminism. In May 2007 a search for *feminism* or *feminist* yields 189 hits, whereas a search for *homosexual* produces 874 hits. (*Lesbian* results in 221 hits and *gay* in 425 hits.) Such anecdotal evidence is in line with the findings of Christian Smith's extensive study of conservative Christians in the United States, which was published in 2000. When asked which groups have too much influence in the United States, only 39 percent of the members of conservative Protestant denominations polled answered "feminists" whereas 68 percent identified "gay rights groups." The percentage of respondents from conservative Christian groups who feel far or very far from feminist groups does not differ significantly from the percentage given by all other Americans. Roughly 29 percent of all Americans—conservative Christians or not—feel a social distance from feminist groups. However, 63 percent of all conservative Christians feel far or very far from homosexuals, compared with 48 percent of all other Americans. In general, Smith's research concludes that one central social issue on which most conservative Christians agree is their penchant for social distance from, and opposition to, homosexuals.[2]

There is an important gender difference in how conservative Christians see same-sex love. Respondents overwhelmingly associate a male figure with homosexuality. The texts of Focus seem more concerned about male homosexuality than about lesbians. In fact, Dobson at times uses the word *homosexual* in a contrast with lesbians, as in the following sentence: "We have never attempted to hurt or ridicule the individual homosexual or lesbian."[3] Likewise, most ordinary Americans associate homosexuality with men. When asked to name the first "homosexual to come to mind" roughly half mentioned a man, and only 23 percent named a woman (the remainder could not think of anyone).[4] At the same time, for conservative Christians, feminism subsumes concerns with lesbianism; and we will see how both are seen as anti-Christian forces aggressively attacking the God-given submissiveness of women. Our next step will be to analyze how male same-sex love appears in Focus texts and then discuss the role of feminism and wifely submission.

In chapter 3 we saw that Dobson's texts appeal to the prior conviction that same-sex love cannot be part of the purview of respectable sexuality. By linking same-sex love to intercourse with donkeys or dogs, they maintain a web of associations in which the love of gays or lesbians appears as utterly reprehensible. Yet Dobson's arguments require that the reader already share the conviction that such love is indeed disgusting and morally toxic. For the members of Evangelical Christian organizations, the morally deficient nature of homosexual acts (and at times people) is self-evident. All that is needed is further recitation of the moral rejection of "the gay lifestyle." This inability to give a reason for the moral and legal rejection of homosexual activity was evident during the oral argument of *Lawrence v. the State of Texas*. Prosecutor Charles Rosenthal, who argued the case in front of the Supreme Court for the State of Texas, was unable to provide an argument as to what is wrong with homosexual conduct in the privacy of one's bedroom. This provoked the following reaction by Justice Stephen G. Breyer: "So what is the justification for this statute, other than, you know, . . . I do not like thee, Doctor Fell, the reason why I cannot tell."[5]

98

We should resist the temptation to declare that Rosenthal's inability to argue for his belief exhibits a lack of intellectual poise. Nobody can argue for statements that seem self-evident. Such claims are not secured by deeper fundamentals to which we can appeal. Rather, the entirety of our practices in words and life supports these basic self-evident claims. The character of Evangelical Christian beliefs about homosexuality as self-evident leads to the communicative impasse witnessed during the Supreme Court trial. Attorney Rosenthal and others who, like him, belief that same-sex love is abhorrent cannot quite communicate their position, and those of us who do not share Evangelical assumptions about homosexuals are left with the question of how to understand them.

Trying to disentangle the logic of some of the conservative Christian claims is not going to be helpful for dissolving this communicative impasse. How should we assess the statement that 75 percent of all gay men ingest feces on a regular basis?[6] Or what is to be said about the idea that there is an impending epidemic of homosexuality? On one hand, part of James Dobson's argument against the idea that homosexuality is inherited is the claim that we can detect epidemics of "homosexuality and lesbianism" and that we are experiencing such an epidemic in today's culture. On the other hand, Focus Web sites state that "the actual number [of homosexuals] is less than three percent."[7] Both statements together make one wonder how a minority population of less than 3 percent can account for an epidemic of homosexuality and lesbianism that destabilizes contemporary Western civilization.

Moreover, a closer look at Dobson's reasoning for assuming that gay and lesbian love undermines society shows a potential argument *supporting* marriage for same-sex couples. Dobson claims that a civilization is threatened "when male and female sexual interests are dispersed and generalized [and when] their effort is invested in the gratification of sensual desires."[8] Therefore, *dispersion* of desire, not the choice of an illicit sexual object, seems to be the root problem, if we follow the logic of Dobson's argument. Out of dispersion of desire arises promiscuity, which Dobson conceives as culturally damaging. Thus, we could extend Dobson's socio-sexual anthropology in the following way: The energy that holds a society together is sexual in nature. When a man is devoted to one man and one family, he is motivated to be productive, innovative, and thrifty on their behalf (the same holds for the union of one man and one woman and of one woman and one woman). Dobson's own anthropology and its focus on dispersion or concentration of desire could give us reasons to endorse marriages for gays and lesbians while rejecting polyamorous relationships.

I mention this point not because I want to argue here for marriage for same-sex couples based on a Dobsonian socio-sexual anthropology. Nor do I want to convince Dobson or convict him of faulty logic. This intellectual exercise rather shows that the textual productions of Focus and organizations like it are best understood not as arguments. As such they would fail. Instead, they are rhetorical constructions. For Dobson, the very association of homosexuality and social chaos is not in need of an argument. This association itself counts as an argument or as a truth to which he can appeal. Thus, instead of reading passages such as these as arguments for the connection between homosexuality and social chaos, I suggest that Dobson's writings function as producing this connection by repeating it over and over again (rhetorical instantiations). The advantage of this suggestion is that instead of blaming him for defective reasoning and puzzling logic, we can begin to understand what is at stake for Dobson's organization.

Let me now describe some key features of the rhetorical production of homosexualities in Focus literature. The following questions are guiding this description: What image of homosexuality is produced in these materials? Who is the homosexual in the world conjured up by these texts? Treating these works like a movie or a morality play, we will find two types of homosexuals among the cast of characters that appear in the texts of Focus on the Family: the hyper-male homosexual and the hypo-male homosexual. Whereas the former appears in the narratives of threat to the Christian community (and is connected with disease, aggression, and abuse) the latter is lacking in male aggressiveness and predatory nature, and he appears only in the narratives of conversion to heterosexuality.

CHRISTIAN MASCULINITY AS CRISIS

One of the many examples for the rhetorical construction of homosexuality in Focus literature is Linda Harvey's *A Checklist to Assess Your School's Risk for Encouraging Homosexuality.*[9] Homosexuality is described as "dangerous" and "risky" behavior and is linked to the spread of HIV and other STDs. Schools that support gay–straight alliance group meetings become "breeding grounds" for homosexuality, and "students' lives and welfare are put at extreme risk." Homosexuality is "dangerous, unhealthy" behavior. By contrast, a school resisting the homosexual agenda "maintains high health standards." This association between health risks and homosexuality is also echoed in the writings of Joseph Nicolosi, one of Focus's psychological experts. "Early self labeling as homosexual or bisexual is one of the top three risk factors for homosexual teen suicide attempts."[10] Finally consider Dobson's comments on the following passage from Paul's letter to the Romans (1:26f): "Men committed indecent acts with other men, and received in themselves the due penalty for their perversion." Dobson asks the reader, "That final sentence sounds like the transmission of sexually transmitted diseases, doesn't it?"[11] Here we can explicitly see the textual leap by which Dobson connects disease with homosexuality. There is no evidence in the text that warrants the move from "due penalty" to "sexual diseases." The connection between the two seems self-evident in his mind, and the repetition aims to strengthen it in the minds of Dobson's readers.

Examples such as these abound in how conservative Christian organizations talk about same-sex love. In the world invoked by these texts, the things that "go along with homosexuality" are suicide, drug use, emotional trauma, and various diseases, such as STDs, AIDS, hepatitis, and cancer. These rhetorical connections aim to naturalize the idea that "homosexuality is ultimately empty and destructive."[12]

THE RHETORICAL CONSTRUCTION OF HOMOSEXUALITIES:
HYPER-MALE AND HYPO-MALE

Homosexuality is associated not only with health risks but moreover with predatory sexuality that targets children and youths. "Sexual promiscuity is undoubtedly rising among students and teachers, and academics are likely to be suffering" at a school where the homosexual agenda is far advanced, states Linda Harvey's aforementioned *Checklist*. Students and their teachers wanting to engage in homosexual behavior will feel encouraged to do so at those schools. A Gay–Straight Alliance Club "provides a venue where students curious about . . . [homosexual] behavior, but who have not yet engaged in it, can readily meet students and even adult advisors to begin homosexual relationships—with school support!" Matt Kaufman, editor of *Boundless* (Focus's publication for collegians), writes, "Having no norms, gay culture also has no real concept of perversion. Even objections to adult–child sex have been relatively recent, tepid and tactical."[13]

In *Bringing Up Boys*, Dobson cites the "vigorous effort by gays to infiltrate the Boy Scouts" as "evidence for the desire [of gays] to gain access to boys." After pointing to a worldwide "effort to lower the age" of consent, Dobson presents as "the most shocking evidence of this targeting of children" the following text: Michael Swift's now infamous "Gay Manifesto," originally published by Boston's *Gay Community News*.[14] Its original introduction reads: "This essay is an outré, madness, a tragic, cruel fantasy, an eruption of inner rage, on how the oppressed desperately dream of being the oppressor."[15] Despite its ironic function (and desperate quality), numerous conservative Christians saw this text as showing the true gay agenda. Swift's text reads in part, "We shall sodomize your sons, emblems of your feeble masculinity, of your shallow dreams and vulgar lies. We shall seduce them in your schools, in your dormitories, in your gymnasiums, in your locker rooms . . . in your youth groups. . . . All churches who condemn us will be closed. Our only gods are handsome young men. . . . Tremble heteroswine when we appear before you without our mask."[16] Dobson comments that he doesn't know whether this manifesto is representative of a larger community. However, he takes from it the lesson that "our boys need to be protected from sexual abuse, whether it is homosexual or heterosexual in character."[17] Why does Dobson devote a full page to quoting the text? This extended recitation of the manifesto would have been unnecessary to make the point that we should protect children from, among other things, heterosexual abuse. The rhetorical function of this page-long quotation is again to re-cite the association of homosexuality with predatory sexual practice.

Implied in the image of predatory sexual practice is a construction of homosexuality as sexuality out of bounds. Linda Harvey's *Checklist* states that the result of accepting a homosexual student club will be that "students accept sexual permissiveness as the norm." Matt Kaufman's article celebrating the courage to come out of homosexuality states under the heading "Risky Business," "Homosexuality is widely associated with behavior best described as compulsive. Numerous studies have found that the average male homosexual is fantastically promiscuous." Homosexuality is further linked here with rampant drug use. The article continues with the now predictable association of danger and disease with homosexuality: "Promiscuity, drug abuse, suicide, HIV—all of them are worst where homosexuality is most accepted."[18]

These excerpts show how the rhetorical construction of *the* homosexual culture or *the* homosexual lifestyle as promiscuous glosses over the question how *individual* homosexual practices (e.g., lesbian practices) relate to *the* culture or lifestyle. Those who engage in homosexual behavior are all subsumed under the lifestyle (singular) or culture independent of their individual choices. Through this rhetorical construction *the* lifestyle assumes an inevitable force overriding the values and choices of individual gays or lesbians. Instead of addressing specific ways of being gay or lesbian, the rhetorical force of the promiscuity recitation is to create the image of a drug-ridden, diseased sexuality out of bounds.

A final important element in this rhetorical recitation of homosexuality is violence. Again, for Dobson the violence of Swift's manifesto proves the destructive nature of the "homosexual agenda." On numerous occasions Dobson portrays his own organization or fellow members of the Christian family as being under verbal and physical attack by gay rights supporters.

Discussing accusations that Focus rhetoric contributed to the murder of Matthew Shepard, Focus and its employees are described as being in turn exposed to hate mail and death threats. Dobson decries the accusations as an "incredible attack on this ministry launched by homosexual activists and their powerful friends in the media." The article goes on to outline the numerous ways in which Christians are under attack in the United States. Dobson finds that "we are moving from a post-Christian era to a decidedly anti-Christian environment. A quick look around will confirm it. A new Broadway play called *Corpus Christi* depicts Jesus as a homosexual who has relations with his apostles and a brief affair with Judas."[19] The interview moves effortlessly from Matthew Shepard's murder to a broad vision of Christian victimization at the hands of a viciously aggressive homosexualized and homosexualizing culture.

The same rhetoric of a victimized church organizes a letter in which Dobson addresses a disaffected gay Christian who wrote to him. First Dobson states his compassionate intentions. He does not want to hurt or ridicule an individual homosexual. In distinction to the individual homosexual whom he does not want to hurt Dobson then introduces *the* homosexual movement. It is only "the more radical elements of the movement" with which he disagrees. In his next rhetorical move in this letter Dobson cites the average income of all "homosexuals" and thus characterizes the power of this homosexual movement in general, not just of its "more radical elements." Finally he contrasts this powerful movement with the victimized position of Christians in the United States.

> You [homosexuals] have Hollywood, the press, the media, the universities, the publishers, the professionals (in the American Bar Association, American Medical Association, etc.), and the judiciary enforcing your "politically correct" agenda. Conservative Christians, by contrast, are stranded pretty

much on their own. Given this undergirding, I hope you can see that our opposition to the gay and lesbian tidal wave is not an expression of hate but one of social justice and common sense.[20]

In this letter we see a remarkable shift of addressees. Dobson moves from talking first to an individual gay person, whom he claims to respect, to then addressing just the "more radical elements" of *the* homosexual movement. Dobson finally addresses "you" homosexuals who are in a position of power as opposed to "us" conservative Christians who struggle. The outcome of this rhetoric is that the individual homosexual is subsumed under the rubric of a powerful aggressive movement. Dobson ends his letter with a list of the "hostilities that have been inflicted on us by the homosexual community and its supporters."[21] Homosexuals threw stones at windows, left bloody animal parts on Focus property, and made bomb threats.

More generally, in discussions of hate crimes, Focus moves to depict homosexual activists as aggressive and threatening and Christians as passive and victimized. One discussion of hate crime legislation quotes Mat Staver, the president of Liberty Counsel, who predicts that homosexuals will not tire until they have reached their goal of being accepted by society. The next sentence reads, "The ultimate agenda is to dominate—not to have tolerance, but to dominate—the worldview, and that worldview is homosexuality."[22]

In the construction of the attacking, dominance-seeking queer we can see in its clearest form the fear of conservative Christians: American values, the American family, and American Christians are subjected to violent attacks by the forces of homosexuality, a homosexuality that, as we already have seen, is associated with the threat of disease, the chaos of drugs and addictive sexual behavior, and the violence of child sexual abuse. Thus, in the world of the Focus texts, we can see two clusters of associations: disease, addiction, lack of freedom, aggression, unfettered sexuality, risky business, impurity, and homosexuality, contrasted with health, freedom, peacefulness, ordered sexuality, childlike helplessness and purity, American family, and Christianity. The American Christian family is thus exposed to the threat of an exploitive, diseased, addictive sexuality.

At this point we can inquire into the gender of this threatening sexuality. Let us analyze the attributes of the threatening cluster (aggression, risky business, and unfettered sexuality) based on Focus's understanding of sexuality.

Women desire a secure, steady, and predictable environment, and they are more cautious. It is in the nature of men to appreciate the risk and adventures of change, writes Dobson. "Boys are designed to be more assertive, audacious and excitable than girls." A real boy tends to risk life and limb and "harasses grumpy dogs. . . . He loves to throw rocks, play with fire, and shatter glass. He also gets great pleasure out of irritating . . . other children. As he gets older, he is drawn to everything dangerous. At around sixteen, he and his buddies begin driving around town like kamikaze pilots on sake. It is a wonder any of them survive."[23] In Dobson's anthropology, boys and men are chemically hard-wired to be risk takers and to be assertive and aggressive. Thus it is not surprising to hear the following advice from Michael Ross, who writes in *Breakaway*, Focus's magazine for boys and "teen-guys," "Accept the fact that your Creator wired you to have an appetite for sex. It truly is a good, healthy God-given thing!"[24] In concert with this, *Brio*, the sister magazine for teenage girls, makes clear that sexual initiative is something that belongs to men. Responding to a girl who wants to ask a young man out, Susi Shellenberger, the advice columnist of *Brio*, states, "Let the guy take the initiative! . . . God designed males to be the head of their household, and to be the provider and caregiver of their family."[25] Although she acknowledges that women must be assertive in their professional lives, she reiterates that women are not to take the active role in sexual or romantic relationships.

Note how these texts combine arguments from natural and divine design. Thus, for Dobson and in the world of the Focus texts, the assertiveness of males and the passivity of females are not only biologically given, they are also theologically mandated. The man is the head, the provider, and the guiding force of the family. Given this understanding of sexuality we can see that the threatening force of out-of-bounds sexuality, which endangers the American family in its childlike purity, is a form of masculine sexuality. In the world evoked by the Focus on the Family texts, the image of the embattled Christian family at the frontiers of civilization is coproduced with the wild hyper-male homosexual embodying a masculinity whose normative sexual and physical aggression and risk taking have gone wild.[26]

The picture of Focus's rhetorical construction of homosexuality is more complex, however. Side by side with the narrative of the hyper-male attack-queer who is pictured as threatening the pure childlike underdog Christians, we find the narrative of the hypo-male gay male. In *Bringing Up Boys*, Dobson begins his chapter on homosexuality with a letter by a gender-confused thirteen-year-old boy who confesses that he behaves and looks like a girl. The letter, which is also widely available through Focus's Web sites, continues by connecting the boy's gender ambiguity with an experience of sexual abuse. An older cousin had exposed himself to the younger boy. The letter writer concludes, "I'm afraid I have a little sodomy in me."[27]

Referring again to Joseph Nicolosi, Dobson states that homosexuality is a "sexual identity disorder" related to "cross-gender behavior." An "effeminate boy" or a "masculinized girl" is in danger of growing into the gay or lesbian lifestyle. In Dobson's world, great care has to be invested so that the affected boys and girls learn the proper gender behavior and become comfortable with their sexual identity. Dobson agrees with Nicolosi that masculinity is not simply given but "an achievement." "Sexual identity disorder" in boys can be prevented only by providing them with stable families and with father figures they can emulate and embrace. "Effeminate boys yearn for what is called 'the three A's.' They are: their father's affection, attention and approval."[28]

In the narrative of the "gender-disorder homosexual" we regularly encounter the tropes of an early rejection in childhood, an absent father, and a lack of a male role model, family chaos in general, insecurity about masculinity, followed by the unhealthy and dangerous morass of gay life.[29] A typical example is the testimony of a former chair of *Exodus International*, John Paulk. On the Web site "Stonewall Revisited" Paulk describes the trajectory of his gay life. He felt different from other boys and rejected by them. When Paulk was four years old his father abandoned the family, leaving him to crave a male presence. Later in his life this craving led Paulk to replace emotional fulfillment with homosexual encounters and to live as a female impersonator. The turning point came when Paulk "met God and He wanted to show me my true identity as a man."[30] The partner story of lesbian sexual identity disorder is written by Anne Paulk (John's wife). Note here again that the threat to ordered sexuality comes from a male.

I wasn't able to say a thing after a teenage boy approached me sexually. Of course, at four years old you're afraid of getting in trouble . . . so you go silent. But inside, the pain of that moment began to grow louder. I became a tomboy. I didn't feel pretty or even lovable. I craved special attention from my dad to make everything all right, but I couldn't tell him why. I began to feel being feminine meant being weak and vulnerable. I didn't know what to do with men . . . they just kept hurting me, so I rejected them.[31]

In this quotation we can see an interesting double bind for normative Christian femininity. Anne Paulk's rejection of her womanhood was related to the perception that "being feminine meant being weak and vulnerable." Embracing her God-given female identity, on the other hand, would mean to accept submissiveness to her husband as the head of the household.

Some Focus Web sites candidly write about the problem of domestic violence in this context. Dobson writes, for example, that submission is not required when the health of the couple or the marriage is at stake. And he cautions that no woman should "tolerate child abuse, child molestation, or wife-beating."[32] We will discuss this in more detail. Here let me note that these texts negotiate the meaning of submission as a field of tensions. On one hand submission is an act of female strength and trust in the face of potential male violence; on the other it is also as an act of handing over power to the potentially abusive husband and to the Lord.

In general, in the context of the narrative of coming out of homosexuality, we encounter over and over again the pleas for compassion: It is important for Christians to understand charitably the confusion that homosexuals are going through because of their sexual identity disorder. The goal is to allow the homosexual to identify with and embrace his or her biologically given and divinely assigned sexual role. Men have to become comfortable being men, to identify with male role models, and women have to become comfortable being women. As we can read in the testimony of the president of Desert-Stream, Andrew Comiskey, "As I continued to grow in my security as a man among other men, I began to feel and think differently towards women. God began to release my heterosexual desires."[33] It is particularly in such stories of sin and healing that we encounter the doll-playing, nonmasculinized hypo-male. The gender-instability gay is linked in the narratives of Focus primarily to stories of Christian conversion.

Given the background of Focus's gender system, we can see that the rhetorical construction of homosexuality produces an image of male homosexuality both as feminine and as overmasculine. Combined with this double construction is a double imperative for gays. On one hand there is the explicit imperative that gays have to become more male and embrace their masculinity. On the other hand—and implied in the rhetorical construction of homosexuality as overaggressive, chaotic, and male—gays have to hold their oversexed all-penetrating masculinity in check. This would seem to be an impossible set of demands. Thus the question arises: What rhetorical work does the double construction of homosexuality perform? Why are there two—and particularly these two—homosexualities?

BETWEEN SCYLLA AND CHARYBDIS

Normative masculinity for Focus is produced in a field of conflicting demands: On one hand, the Christian man has to assume his masculine role by being aggressive and by asserting sexual initiative. Moreover, he has to live up to the demands on his sexual role as head of the household to whom the wife has to submit. At the same time the man has to be submissive to Jesus Christ and the commandments of the "boss," God. As Dobson writes, "We must begin with the presupposition that the universe has a Boss, and He has defined the dimensions of right and wrong in immutable terms."[34] In fact, the universe, the family, and society are structured through cascading submissions. Consider how advice author Heather Koerner explains the status of political authority. As a citizen Koerner obeys these authorities not because they are moral, right, or responsible "but because God has placed these authorities over me. This submission is seen over and over again in the Word. A wife is to submit to her husband, even if he is an unbeliever. Children are to submit to their parents, slaves to their masters, and all of us to submit to one another out of reverence for Christ."[35] Christian masculinity is embedded in this flow of submission. Yet given Focus's understanding of sexuality, the Christian man has to be powerful and vulnerable, aggressive and submissive, and thus both masculine and feminine. He has to be male in relation to his wife, his family, and the outside world. And he has to be submissive, passive, and receptive in relation to God.

Normative Christian masculinity is therefore constructed through conflicting sexual imperatives such as the following: "Be aggressive and be a man! But don't be too rebellious, too aggressive, or too chaotic, lest your masculinity get out of bounds." (The warnings against child abuse and domestic violence in the context of the discourse of female submissiveness show how the rhetorical construction of normative Christian manhood is closely linked to images of a destructive form of sexuality.) The second, conflicting command to Christian men can be paraphrased as "Be receptive and passive toward God and be submissive (as a woman is submissive to her husband)! But don't be too passive and too receptive, lest you lose your masculinity."

The rhetorical construction of both homosexualities is therefore located in the rhetorical production of normative masculinity. Consider the following observation of Heather Hendershot at a True Love Waits conference promoting abstinence among conservative Christian teens:

> Girls and boys were taught about chastity in separate seminars. . . . Boys . . . were directed to loudly chant "We are real men! We are real men!" They were told that abstinence was not emasculating, that "Adam was a real man," and that the Garden of Eden housed "Adam and Eve," not "Adam and Steve." The problem of how one could be "a real man" and a virgin was solved by asserting homophobic machismo. Ironically, in order to control the male body, to save it from its own heterosexual aggression, that body must be constructed as aggressively heterosexual and masculine.[36]

In my reading, both types of homosexuality present the feared alternative positions into which normative Christian manhood could devolve. The overaggressive homosexual is in rebellion against the divine will and natural order. Citing this image of chaotic maleness over and over again thus instantiates the normative vision of submissiveness. The gay hypo-male presents the opposite danger for the normative Christian male. Normative Christian masculinity has to embrace the natural and divinely ordained aggressiveness and assertiveness. The hyper- and the hypo-male homosexual are therefore construed as the Scylla and Charybdis between which the normative male Christian traveler has to find his way.

SUBMISSION AND THE CRISIS OF CHRISTIAN WOMANHOOD

SUBMISSION BETWEEN AGENCY AND VULNERABILITY

As I mentioned at the beginning of this chapter, the texts of Focus on the Family are less concerned with lesbians than they are with gay men. In general, women who love women are rarely a topic in Christian Right discourse. If lesbians are mentioned at all, they are depicted either as "gay-lesbians" or as "feminist-lesbians." The "gay-lesbians" show allegedly how lesbian desire leads to a loss of femaleness. Gay-lesbians are over-sexed, anarchic, disease-ridden, and predatory just like the hyper-male. They show "unnatural" sexual initiative. As one informant for Didi Herman's *The Anti-Gay Agenda* put it, "As the attacks on what I would call the normal sexual roles continue . . . you see even within the lesbian side of this thing terms like bull-dyke . . . that tend to represent a male-oriented, female lesbian." According to the convictions of not only this informant, women are by nature gentler and more nurturing than men. Yet *even* lesbians have lost their sense for natural womanhood. Instead of an encounter of "natural" female sexualities, lesbian desire is presented as disordered because it follows a masculine model. As we already saw in the testimony of Anne Paulk, lesbians in the world of Focus on the Family show uneasiness with their female identity. Consequently they have to relearn what it means to be truly female. The same is true for the figure of the "lesbian feminist," who is imagined as a woman who rejects all things male. Revealingly, another of Herman's sources states that we "see that lesbianism is but the logical end-result of feminist autonomism, which, pushed further, leads to the glorification of masturbation as self-assertion and freedom from males, to self-insemination, and to single parenthood as the crowning liberty." The lesbian feminist or feminist lesbian is "at war with motherhood, femininity, family and God," and paradoxically she is male in her "anti-male militancy."[37] In a similar vein, a text on submission in *Boundless*, Focus's magazine for college-age men and women, states that rejecting submission is the result of women who are pursuing a "vendetta against men." These women are engaged in this power struggle because of feminism. "Feminism, while accomplishing many good things, has unfortunately thrown men and women into the bullring, pitted against each other."[38]

In sum, the roles of lesbians and feminists in the world of conservative Christian texts overlap. They are women who refuse to submit under the rightful authority of male headship and oppose the divinely ordained cascade of submission. For Christian men, submitting to the Lord was meant to be an effort that keeps an allegedly natural male aggressiveness in check (or to boost that aggression if needed); women, on the other hand, are considered to be naturally more submissive. They are called to resist the cultural forces of feminism that make women overly aggressive and thus distort the image of "true" womanhood.

However, as Anne Paulk's testimony describes, submission does not mean a complete lack of initiative. This misunderstanding drove her to become a "tomboy" because she thought (wrongly, according to Focus) that "being feminine meant being weak and vulnerable." Again, her inability to embrace the role of submissive wife had to do with the experience of sexual violence. Indeed, such violence is an important foil against which both Dobson and Focus on the Family describe submission. (Countless family advice manual discussions of submission are filled with concerns about Christian men who abuse their wives.[39] Yet only a very small minority of Evangelical authors explore any connection between the rhetoric of male headship, wifely submission, and domestic violence.[40]) In *Brio* we read that "a guy's love is never true if he forces a girl into sexual situations. For an abuser, the act of sex isn't a way to show love. Instead, it's a way to force submission to gain control. Only in a mutually loving marriage can sex be explored in a healthy and safe manner."[41] Submission cannot be forced; it has to be actively given.

The concerns about male aggression are not surprising, given what we have heard about how Focus conceives of normative Christian masculinity. Recalling how Dobson talks about the "sheer biological power of sexual desire in a male" and the "feminine inertia" when it comes to sex, Bartkowski comments, "If his female readers haven't already gotten the message about their sexual obligations within the marital relationship [he] warns them explicitly that 'abstinence is usually more difficult for men to tolerate' and adds that men who are not treated to frequent sex at home may look outside the marital relationship to have their sexual needs met."[42] Marital advice manuals are full of the recommendation that the wife needs to make herself completely available to her husband's (normatively insatiable) sexual desires. Evangelist Beverly LaHaye famously warns that women who show much assertiveness and initiative may "demasculinize a man by dominating and leading him in everything—including sex."[43] Echoes of this warning that female assertiveness leads to the masculinization of women abound in current Focus literature. Dana Ryan, a columnist for *Boundless*, writes in an article about the Christian understanding of submission that women who reject the idea of submission also "complain about weak men." Rejecting submission somehow leads to the weakening of the male. In submission, women have to find a balance between the degree to which they give in and accept the male's greater aggressiveness for the sake of their marriage and their own safety from abuse. Again, Dana Ryan states that biblical submission does not constitute tyranny because Christian men are called to love their wives, just as Jesus loved his Church. The ideal man is Jesus, who gave his life for the church. "I don't know of any woman who wouldn't want to be loved by a man who was willing to die for her. And if a man were willing to die for his wife, would she not naturally love and respect him in return?"[44]

According to these texts, submission does not mean that women have no agency; rather, through a husband's love women learn how God loves them and the church. "I know God's view of how women should be treated because of my husband. He tries to follow the Bible's command to love me as Christ loves the church. Think about this. Christ doesn't oppress the church. He isn't forceful or unkind to His bride. He was willing to be crucified because of His love for the church."[45] Indeed, there are passages in Focus's publications endorsing mutual submission. Again in *Boundless* we read that "the biblical admonition to submit applies to everyone," demanding that the couple respect each other and be willing to sacrifice for the partner. All this will create "love and consequently a desire to submit."[46]

SUBMISSION BETWEEN EQUALITY AND AUTHORITY

Submission is something both partners must engage in, submission is something that is natural for women, and women are called to submit to their husband's authority: In conservative Christian elite texts about the proper biblical understanding of submission, ideals of equality are mixed in with those of sexual hierarchies and masculine authority. And it is important to note that this is true even for texts from a single organization, such as Focus, which stresses the natural and essential difference between the sexes.

Let us consider closely the logic of an article on submission by Kimberly Rae, the Christian missionary: Explaining why the Bible states the husband should be the head of the household, she uses the metaphor of the team to declare that the husband has to make the final decision in matters of the family. Without a leader a team will be unproductive because individual team members will either be inactive or act without coordination with one another. "A family is a team, and in any team somebody has to be responsible for the final decisions."[47]

The wife as team player, or executive vice president, or second in command—these tropes are used in conservative Christian literature to make clear that she has to subordinate herself into a clear line of command. Although this does not imply that she has no authority, the wife has to obey her husband's wishes, or the entire family will fail. Thus Rae's texts echoes the Christian family manuals from the 1970s that stated that once the husband made a decision, the team has to work together to implement it. "In this relationship, they share a oneness, a good communication, emotional peace and security, *provided the vice president is not struggling to gain control.*"[48] Through these analogies, the marital relationship is clearly hierarchized.

Is this a logically necessary move? Yes, it may be plausible that a team needs a leader, but does this requirement extend to a couple? Is it impossible for a Christian couple to share decisions and responsibility? As in the post-revolutionary marriage ideal we encountered in chapter 3, an emphasis on a clear line of command seems to outweigh the romantic ideal of equality. Thus it is important to keep the team players in their rightful places. Women are admonished to not struggle for control beyond their station. Similar to the discourse of respectability, submission is a conceptual tool to establish socially acceptable hierarchies. Whereas respectability establishes a middle-class hierarchy vis-à-vis the working class, submission stratifies the marriage relationship from within.

But let us return to Rae's article in *Brio*. The executive authority of the husband does not mean that the wife has no voice in the family's decision-making process. The team leader should not abuse his authority and quash all discussions. Rather, he must make the final decision. Rae concludes, "Submission? Basically, women aren't supposed to be bossy, naggy or manipulative."[49]

Let me point out here the logical difference between being bossy, naggy, and manipulative on one hand and never being allowed to make a final call on the other. Accepting that neither party in the couple should be bossy does not imply that only one of them is allowed to be the decider in the family. It is not hard to imagine a couple in which neither partner is manipulative and both make decisions jointly. In other words, the admonition not to be bossy in Rae's text, like the reminder that the vice president should not struggle for power, describes the attitude that women should assume in the face of their husband's headship. The content of submission according to this Christian missionary is that the husband has the authority to decide what is best for the couple and the family. The attitude of normative submission demands from Christian women that they accept this content without resentment. Rather, they should cultivate an attitude of gently trusting the decision of their God-given leader. Rae writes that her husband does respect her opinions precisely because she is not insisting on them. Her attitude is that although she does not always get her way, her life's work is to do what God wants.[50]

Without this proper attitude, wives will lose the ear and respect of their husbands and potentially weaken their masculinity by competing with them for the power to make decisions. Thus implied in seemingly commonsense advice about mutual respect are strong messages aimed at disciplining the ideal Christian wife to accept her husband's authority. If the communication between the couple works well, then this is a sign of God's providential cooperation of the sexes. If communication breaks down, according to these texts, the wives may need to be less nagging and power grabbing.

From these observations we can see that even in texts from a single organization submission appears as a tension-filled practice. Ideals of mutuality and equality coexist in Focus's discourse on submission with those of a strict chain of command and sexual hierarchy in the life of the couple. In descriptions of the ideal of submission, women are admonished to avoid a desire for too much authority and independence and to resist thinking of themselves as weak and powerless. Again, we see that the sexual ideal for the Christian woman is constructed along conflicting imperatives: Be submissive, but not too much, lest you invite abuse and think of yourself as weak. Assume a posture of authority, but not too much, lest you compete with your husband for power and turn into a lesbian–gay–feminist. Consequently, the meaning of submission for the daily practice for the Christian family is to be constantly negotiated.

COMPLICATED FLOWS OF POWER IN ORDINARY FAMILY LIFE

Importantly, these tensions in what constitutes submission are not confined to elite discourses, as Gallagher observes. "Ordinary evangelicals certainly struggle in their effort to reconcile these apparently contradictory ideals [of authority and equality]." Consider the following woman's effort to work through how she is both equal and not equal to her husband:

> You're equal in the sight of God, but in the relationship of the family he is more equal than I am. You know, he's the head. So I guess you can't say we're equal because I don't have equal authority as far as the family relationship goes. Although when he's not there, I deal with things. I don't know; it's kind of hard to explain. . . . Well, we're equals in that I'm not in an inferior position in the family. With the kids, my word goes as well as his word. . . . So my authority is as good as his; it's just . . . when it comes to push and shove, he has to be [the head]. I have to submit to him as the supreme authority in the family.[51]

Let me note that this woman is not alone in her assessment that she as a wife would give in on a contested decision. Gallagher shows that most Protestant women, regardless of denominational background, report that they are more likely to do so in a conflict. They do not need a doctrine of submission or headship to tell them that acquiescing in a contested situation is expected from them. Nearly half of all mainline Protestant men, but only 31 percent of all women of these denominations, claim that both partners are equally likely to give in. Fifty percent of the mainline women state that they are most likely to submit to their husband's wishes. The wives and husbands of these denominations do not agree on who compromises in conflicts in their marriages. On the other hand, Evangelical men and women, as well as liberal Protestant couples, are more in agreement about how contested decisions are made. Roughly 20 percent of both men and women think that the husbands and 40 percent that the wives are more likely to give in; around 33 percent of either sex state that both partners are equally likely to accept their partner's decision. Independent of their different theologies of sexual and family relations, both liberal and Evangelical Protestants agree in their assessment of how conflicts are de facto solved in the family. In short, it is not clear what the discourse of submission amounts to in the daily decision-making processes of Evangelical couples.[52]

Studies about individual Evangelical congregations show likewise that the flows of power between the sexes are complicated in communities and families alike. In *God's Daughters*, Marie Griffith describes how members of one particular Evangelical ministry for women, Aglow, subscribe to the idea that the act of submission actually empowers them. Through this practice they tap into the power of the Spirit.

> For the Spirit-filled women of Aglow transformation encompasses a broad variety of meanings: victory over sin and sickness, whether physical, emotional, or spiritual; the uncovering and/or restoration of the authentic, hidden self; a surrender of the selfish will in favor of God's plan; finding new love in Jesus, whether as father, lover, or friend; the ecstasy wrought by the infusion of the Holy Spirit, accompanied with feelings of freedom, liberation, and power.[53]

The sense of being empowered by the Spirit is an essential part of the narratives of Aglow women who struggle with the burdens of sickness, economic stresses, and addiction. It allows them to accept what they cannot change and to find meaning and providence in events that otherwise would be evidence of life's utter capriciousness.

Despite this language of female power, even for a women's ministry such as Aglow it is important to tread carefully when it comes to women in leadership roles. When the organization changed its bylaws to allow women to serve on the national advisory board in 1993, this news was kept secret, for fear the Aglow members and their supporters would object.[54] The degree to which women are allowed to occupy leadership positions in the church and to be pastors is also debated in the Southern Baptist convention and in many Evangelical churches around the country.[55]

At the same time, conservative Christian women have the power to shape, undermine, or protect their husband's masculinity. Given that male aggression must be checked and controlled through marriage, women have the responsibility and the power to shape good Christian men. Echoing the works of Phyllis Schlafly and other family advice writers, Aglow women are convinced of the responsibility of the wife to uphold their husband's Christian virility. "It is up to her to see that her man is kept satisfied, as well as contained, assuring him of his worth by admiring his virility."[56] Women therefore have the task to tame an otherwise destructive male energy and steer men toward forming and protecting a healthy Christian family. This is an idea we have already encountered in Dobson's thoughts on marriage as the place where men's natural aggressiveness is channeled into socially beneficial cooperation. Indeed, as Griffith and others note, in many of the texts on wifely submission, the husband's ego and masculinity come across as being very fragile and constantly endangered. Without the constant encouragement of their wives, men lose their masculinity and become weaklings, or they spin into chaos and turn into abusers. Thus we see in the discussion about submission a set of complex gender images: Men are fragile, morose, yet also dangerous and women are active, strong, and caring.[57] After our discussion of the hyper- and hypo-male homosexual, this conflicted picture of masculinity should be familiar. Submission is not only a strategy for the domestication of men but also a way to keep women provided for (by making their husbands responsible) and safe (by preventing their men from becoming abusers).

In sum, the idea that the sexes are equal in their dignity but not similar in their authority because of their different natures is difficult to understand even for Evangelical Christians themselves. Gallagher quotes Evangelical author Rebecca Groothuis, who, from the perspective of biblical feminism, assesses the conservative Christian rhetoric of authority and equality as follows: "Regardless of how hierarchicalists try to explain the situation, the idea that women are equal *in* their being, but unequal *by virtue of* their being, is contradictory."[58]

Despite these ambiguities in submission or headship, the ideal of husbandly leadership has to be maintained in both elite discourse and in how ordinary Evangelicals talk about their family structure. Husbands and wives in both dual- and single-income families overwhelmingly state that the man should be the head of the household. It is true that husbands who have working wives are less likely to think of themselves as the final authority (50.9%) than those who are the sole income provider (79%). According to Gallagher, this suggests that the sense of male authority is indeed undermined by women's employment outside the house, "as LaHaye and Dobson have long argued. Yet this sense of diminished authority is something we find only among men, not women. Wives in single- and dual-income households do not significantly differ in supporting the idea that husbands should be the final authority." Indeed, most Evangelicals think that they have equal responsibilities in parenting decisions, and there is no correlation between gender ideology and participation in ordinary household tasks. In fact, mainline (45%) and liberal (39%) Protestant men are more likely than Evangelicals to think that their wives have more responsibility for parenting.[59]

Although being neither the sole breadwinner nor the final decider defines headship for all Evangelicals, more than 90 percent agree that the husband is the "spiritual leader."[60] In fact, 63 percent of male Evangelical respondents say that they have more responsibilities for their family's spiritual lives than their wives. Yet 45 percent of women state that they have more responsibility, compared to 34 percent who think their husbands have it. In comparison with other Protestant denominations we find that Evangelical men are significantly more likely to claim that they have an important role to play in their family's spiritual lives. Only 29 percent of liberal and 34 percent of mainline Protestant men assume that this area of life is their responsibility. The language of headship seems to be aimed at and successful in convincing Evangelical men that they have a role to play in their families when it comes to child rearing and to religion. Yet in their daily lives Evangelical men and women distinguish between the husband's ideal responsibility for their family and his actual engagement in the family. "In the end, being, not doing is the essence of male leadership in evangelical homes," particularly in the realm of the family's spiritual well-being and somewhat less so in that of parenting.[61]

A structure of sexual being is therefore at stake. Confusing this structure leads to emasculated men and masculinized women. Thus, the symbolic nexus of final authority, leadership in the family, and masculinity in contrast to feminine receptivity is the center of the debates about sexuality— in short, the establishing of a specific heterosexual gender difference characterized by the cascade of submission.

In the end there is theoretical (and practical) confusion about what constitutes the right way to organize the relationship of the sexes. Instead of providing a clear blueprint for marital relationships, "submission" is a composite concept that aims to hold together conflicting values: the romantic equality of the partners and the respectable hierarchy of subordination of women under men.

The image of the disreputable feminist or gay lesbians and their cultural allies represent the feared possibility that women reject their place in the hierarchy of gender and the cascade of submission. Weak men and a disturbed social order will result. The image of the abused woman, on the other hand, establishes a difference between submission enforced by violence and voluntary acquiescence to male authority.

The threat of abuse is real, and it is acknowledged in Focus literature. Given the insistence that male sexuality is by nature bordering on the violent and that women need to make themselves sexually available to their husbands, submission can never be without danger for women. The stories of John and Anne Paulk, mentioned previously, therefore exhibit an eerie truth: Becoming a submissive Christian wife is fraught with the risk of entering an abusive relationship. Becoming a Christian man and husband implies endorsing a vision of masculinity full of aggression. The ideal picture of the complementary cooperation of the sexes, which is ubiquitous in conservative Christian texts, is painted over a darker vision of sexual violence and danger. By nature men are dangerous and need to be constrained, and by nature women are receptive and passive. Only if both sexes order themselves according to the cascade of theologically mandated submissions can chaos be prevented. Men have to submit to "their boss," as Dobson stated, women to God and to their husbands, children to their parents, and families to the political authorities.

At the same time it is unclear in theory and practice what constitutes the right meaning of submission or the right amount of aggression for men or passivity for women. Thus we do not find a stable concept but a field of constant negotiations and struggles at the center of this Christian sexual theology. This field of contestation is delineated by figures such as the anti-male feminist, the gay-lesbian, the hyper-male attack queer, or the hypo-male homosexual. Constructing these characters is part of a strategy of projecting allegedly clear sexual and theological boundaries. Yet the rhetorical construction of these transgressive sexual identities does not function as a cover over an otherwise confused picture of sexual relations. Rather, these images engender the confusion and the complex negotiations of power, divinity, and sexuality in which conservative Christians are engaged, which they share with a wider American public.

Chapter 3 showed how conservative Christian language about marriage for same-sex couples is connected to a broader tradition of respectability, romance, and the American polity. In particular, we learned that for conservative Christians, marriage is mandated theologically and socially to unite society on the basis of a specific understanding of the ideal heterosexual gender and sexual difference. Here we have analyzed the role that the rhetorical production of different male homosexualities and of the feminist and gay lesbian played in constructing these ideal Christian sexualities. Christian masculinity and femininity are not stable identities but are held in a constant state of crisis, potentially disintegrating into abuse and transgressive sexual behavior. In the next chapter we will explore further the theological underpinnings of these sexualities as crisis. It is true that, as Gallagher argues, talk about submission establishes a boundary for conservative Christian culture. The ability to embrace true biblical submission is seen as a hallmark of Christians who reject the undue influence of feminism and secularism in family and state. For example, Dana Ryan is surprised that even in her Christian college some women are influenced by a feminist rejection of submission.[62] Yet we also saw that the cascades of submissions are connected to ideas about God and about political authority. In the final chapter we will explore these theologico-political connections further. I will argue that the unstable meanings of Christian masculinity and femininity enable a productive form of crisis: It makes the Christian bodies into a landscape where the tensions of self-power and other-power are played out, tensions that are typical for many Christian visions of grace.

A POLITICAL AND SEXUAL THEOLOGY OF CRISIS

Why is the issue of same-sex love so deeply problematic for conservative Christian groups and their followers? What motivates their nearly obsessive concern with it? After the analysis of the previous chapters we can see the outlines of an answer for these questions. The invocation of the hyper- or hypo-male gay, the masculinized lesbian, or the secular feminist woman helps delineate normative Christian heterosexuality as one that is structured by a hierarchy of submission. Thus, the Christian imagination of same-sex love and of feminism plays an important part in the construction of respectable sexual relations. As we learned in chapter 3, respectability is an important ingredient of the American marriage ideal. On this point, the rhetoric of organizations such as Focus on the Family and the history of the American marriage agree. Romance is not enough to build a middle-class nation. The institution of romantic and respectable marriage is conceived of as the foundation of American society, and it helps discipline its citizenry. Respectable marriage is the place where the state's care for itself shapes the inner life of its subjects and their structure of desire. And indeed, defending the American marriage means defending the heterosexual difference, one that many conservative Americans and Christians understand as being defined by the aforementioned cascade of submission.

We have seen that this cascade was meant to represent the allegedly clear flows of authority from the husband to the wife, from the government to the citizenry, and from God to humanity. Thus the ideal of a patriarchal nation based on masculine authority with clear lines of command and clear demands of submission lies at the heart of conservative Christian discourse on sexuality, religion, and politics. And our analysis in chapter 4 showed how the specific images of gay and lesbian sexuality disseminated in conservative Christian texts represented attempts to delineate this patriarchal ideal. The characterization of lesbian and gay sexualities as defying the order of submission (or struggling to align themselves with it, in the case of the hypo-male) helped outline the empty center of normative Christian sexuality. This strategy is necessary precisely because it is unclear in theory and practice what constitutes the right relationship between authority and submission in normative Christianity.

The theoretical and practical confusion about what the language of the husband's "servant leadership" or the Christian wife's submission means raises the following questions: What purpose do the references to the patriarchal flow of power and authority serve for conservative Christians, and how do these religious and sexual ideals relate to the wider American culture? We will conclude our analysis in this chapter by addressing these questions. Going beyond a mere functionalist explanation for the Christian language of headship and submission, I will continue my argument that the tensions of Christian sexuality produce the Christian life as an embodied struggle. What is natural sexuality? What is the right kind of human agency in the drama of salvation? And how does our erotic life relate to the divine? Instead of finding clear answers the conservative Christian is drawn into a vortex of unstable meanings, which generates the need for constant embodied (i.e., sexual) struggle for the right Christian life. In the second part of this chapter I will argue that this tension-filled normative Christian sexuality is not countercultural. Rather, its ideals of masculine theological and sexual power and female submission are well anchored in middle-class American gender practices. Conservative Christian language about same-sex love connects with and reinforces the shaping of middle-class sexualities in their normative distributions of power.

BEYOND FUNCTIONALISM

Gallagher and Smith argue that the theology of the husband's leadership has little relevance for how ordinary Christians arrange their marital relations. They are as egalitarian as other Americans in resolving disputes and organizing household tasks, as we have seen. If there is any impact of such rhetoric at all, conservative Christian language about family values seems to make husbands more involved in their family, compared with mainstream Protestants. Gallagher concludes that the language of husbandly leadership functions not so much as an ideal to be emulated by conservative Christian couples as a marker to define the boundaries of the Evangelical subculture. Their marital arrangements do not differ from those of other Americans when it comes to how decisions are made, for example. Yet, the language of headship and submission allows Evangelicals to feel separated from the American mainstream. Embrace the language of submission (even if you don't quite know what it means) and you are in; reject it and you are influenced by anti-Christian secular and feminist thought.[1]

This explanation analyzes conservative Christian language of patriarchal authority in terms of its social function, that is, its capacity to delineate the boundaries of a social group. Although this is an important element, we are left to wonder about the theological and political vision implied in the ideal of husbandly leadership. For example, the few conservative Christian students at my rather liberal university who confided in me their aim to become submissive wives clearly set themselves apart from their peers. Yet I doubt that it is just their desire to live in a subculture that motivates them to embrace the conviction that "submission" is an important goal in a person's marital and spiritual life. Consider as a thought experiment the merits of the functionalist argument in another example: Professing one's desire for a same-sex relationship clearly sets a person apart, yet it seems incorrect to follow from this fact that such a desire is motivated solely by the wish to be different. Gallagher realizes that more is going on and describes very briefly the theological ideals connected to headship. These are the themes of divine authority and the hierarchy of the created cosmos.

What sets the majority of Evangelicals apart is the countercultural idea that men are leaders and women are subordinate partners within marriage. It is not just that husband should be the head of the household. After all, 60 to 80 percent of other religiously committed Protestants believe the same. What is distinctive is that headship, centered on men's spiritual leadership, reflects a nonnegotiable, God-given spiritual hierarchy established in creation.[2]

The focus on hierarchies that are based in the divinely ordained world order is held in tension with ideals of equality and mutuality, as we have seen. Gallagher notes that this is a productive tension for conservative Christians. It allows them to be both similar to the American mainstream, by supporting egalitarian values, and different from it, by holding onto the idea of headship. Moreover, most Evangelicals perceive that to make a good marriage work, they need a balance between a clear hierarchization of the sexes on one hand and a sense of equality between them on the other hand. Using the vocabulary of our inquiry, they need both romance and stratifying respectability in their relationships.

Given our analysis of the American marriage in chapter 3, I see, in contrast to Gallagher, not a strategy of differentiation but one of alignment with the American mainstream. The intense debates about allowing same-sex couples to marry have shown how a Christian discourse of heterosexual stratification is important in the eyes of the American public for the formation of respectable unions. The desire to live in a society structured by a sexual hierarchy of submission and to anchor claims of authority in some cosmic order seems to resonate well with many Americans. Conservative Christians express this desire for a stratified sexual order perhaps more aggressively or intently than other Americans. More specifically, the language of headship or submission, which is familiar to them, allows these Christians to make explicit the conflicts inherent in America's sexual hierarchies. This language is part of the conservative Christian dialect (to remind us of the definitional discussion from chapter 1), which makes such Christians recognizable to each other. Yet, this dialect also addresses a complex of conflicting themes that concern the American mainstream.

In the following I want to explore these tensions in three steps, first by examining the idea that nature stabilizes the sexual order in the world imagined by conservative Christian texts, second by analyzing the conundrum of the relationship between divine and human agency in the drama of salvation, and third by turning to reflections on the nature of divinity itself.

STRUGGLING FOR THE CHRISTIAN LIFE

NATURE AS CRISIS

In numerous texts, conservative Christian organizations repeat that the character of the sexes is anchored in nature. Biology and anatomy tell us what it means to be man and determine the divinely approved sexual identity. As one female advice columnist writes, "The physical structure of the female would tell us that woman was made to receive, to bear, to be acted upon, to complement, to nourish."[3]

126

The story is more complicated, however. As we have seen, the rhetorical constructions of homosexualities in the world of Focus exhibited a deep uneasiness about the foundations of sex and sexual behavior. On one hand, boys are boys, and they are hardwired to assume their natural and God-given roles. "The sexes were carefully designed by the Creator to balance one another's weakness and meet one anther's needs." And Dobson explicitly states that "what it means to be masculine and why 'boys are a breed apart'" is determined by "testosterone, serotonin and the amygdales." However, Focus on the Family texts also state that masculinity is an achievement, and growing up straight takes work.[4] If what it means to be a man is biologically determined, and if male and heterosexual desires and behaviors are hardwired into our bodies, then there should be little room for achieving masculinity, nor should there be room for feminizing men or for luring them into homosexuality. Indeed, Dobson writes that the feminist agenda of "whimpifying" men will never succeed because "it contradicts masculine nature."[5] What we are as men or women is deeply engrained in our biology, so much so that we can never be changed in our sexual identities. "Many men—not just those who were taught to be inexpressive—find it difficult to match the emotions of their wives. They *cannot* be what their women want them to be," writes Dobson in *Straight Talk: What Men Need to Know. What Women Should Understand.* And he illustrates this general principle with the case of a good Christian man who tried to change his attitude toward expressing himself. "He has tried to rearrange his basic nature on five or six occasions, but to no avail. A leopard cannot change his spots, and an unromantic, uncommunicative man simply cannot become a sensitive talker."[6] At the same time, there is a great fear that through the influence of secular American culture men will become feminized and women will become masculinized. If masculinity were a given trait, like the spots on a leopard, then such a fear would be baseless. This worry would be akin to being afraid that a secular culture might influence whether our children will have opposable thumbs.[7] I understand these conflicting messages as expressing and performing a deep uneasiness about the reliability of nature in providing a theologically acceptable sexuality. Far from being an unassailable basis from which to deduce the correct meaning of sexuality, nature is a complicated and problematic reality. As in the case of reading scripture, deciphering what is written in the book of nature is both easy and perplexingly difficult.

We have already seen that ideal Christian masculinity is composed of a complicated mixture of natural aggression and Christian virtuous restraint (made possible through the wife's submission). Left alone, masculinity, which is allegedly inherently aggressive, leads to destructive effects. Its natural aggression must be channeled to socially constructive ends through the cultural institution of marriage. Ideal Christian femininity consists likewise of balancing an alleged inborn passivity with the right amount of initiative. Focus's dramatic vision of the need for sexual complementarity presupposes a split between the civilizing effects of human culture and the potentially destructive energies of unbridled sexual nature. Again, if the cooperation between the sexes were as natural as developing the ability to pick up a flower with a pincer formed by thumb and index finger, there would be little room for the civilizing forces of culture.

As the analysis in chapter 4 showed, right Christian masculinity and femininity are defined not by a clear concept of essential sexual features but by conflicting demands and contradictory dynamics. Thus side by side with language about the immutability and clarity of sexual characteristics we find a profound instability of meaning. This fluidity generates the need for constant negotiations of what constitutes the outline of the right Christian

127

sexuality. Although the center of this sexuality is empty, its contours are established with the help of the outlandish images of gay and lesbian sexualities.

This placement of the rhetorical construction of gays, lesbians, or feminists and their function within the construction of natural sexuality has surprising resonances with the work of feminist philosopher Judith Butler. In *Bodies That Matter*, Butler writes that "sexual difference . . . is never simply a function of material differences, which are not in some way both marked and formed by discursive practices."[8] The allegedly natural biological differences between men and women are produced in the context of linguistic and thus regulatory practices. The meaning of heterosexuality is not simply given. Rather, we create cultural practices in which this sexual binary is invoked, validated, or questioned. Because there is no unambiguous material grounding for the sexual differences, these regulated (and regulating) practices are in need of constant repetition and re-citation.

> "Sex" is an ideal construct which is forcibly materialized through time. It is not a simple fact or a static condition of a body, but a process whereby regulatory norms materialize "sex" and achieve this materialization through a forcible reiteration of these norms. That this reiteration is necessary is a sign that materialization is never quite complete, that bodies never quite comply with the norms by which their materialization is impelled.[9]

The meanings of masculinity or femininity are not stabilized through essential features of bodies or things out there. Not some *thing* but a web of stabilizing discourses establishes what we understand masculinity or femininity to be. These stabilizing discourses are also in need of stabilization. Therefore, in order to have a steady experience of the world, we must re-create over and over again these stabilizing discursive structures. This need for reiteration points to the profound instability of our sexual order, which is the result of the fact that there is no underlying material basis that grounds our discourses about masculinity or femininity. Therefore, the constant mentioning of homosexualities in the discourse of Focus is part of the necessary recreation of the discursive construction of normative Christian heterosexuality. Seen in this framework, the nearly obsessive recitation of the construction of gays and lesbians makes sense. Christians cannot simply point to the thing (by saying *this* is a man) to establish what marks Christian masculinity, but they have to constantly recite its boundaries. The same is true for Christian femininity, it is not a material essence that anchors its meaning but the repetitive description of its borders.

To further this line of analysis, let me turn to instances where the texts of Focus on the Family talk in an explicitly theological fashion about human nature. In connection with lived homosexual desires we find the images of a nature that has fallen into godless chaos, hence the allusions to paganism and chaotic lives and sexualities in the construction of both feminism and homosexuality. The values that sustain the family "are continually exposed to the wrath of hell itself."[10] Theologically speaking, the so-called homosexual and feminist agendas are associated with a fundamental corruption of nature. In the construction of the homosexual or the feminist gender and sex disturbances, we see nature as fundamentally corrupted by rebellion and sin. This threat to God's cosmic order reveals at the same time the instability of nature. What appeared to be eternally stable can be thrown into chaos by the forces of sin and evil. Behind the appearance of a fixed order of nature we find therefore a world threatened to disintegrate into chaos at every step. The texts of Focus construct a double vision of nature: There is nature corrupted, and there is nature redeemed to its original design. Where lived same-sex desire represents the corruption of nature, the narratives of "ex-gays" and the hypo-male homosexual show us the possibility to redeem ourselves by assuming our God-given natural sexualities. In the textual struggles surrounding lesbian and gay love, we see on one hand nature cast in the image of sin and, on the other hand, nature as re-created by God. The Christian life appears then as a passage from one form of nature to the other.

It is thus not surprising to find this double vision of nature at another place in the world of Focus (a place that does not deal with homosexuality at all), namely in Heather Jamison's article "Pursuing Holiness in Marriage." She describes marriage as a struggle for forgiveness and for holiness. "Holiness means that we are to become different from our natures, which have nursed us and comforted us. Our perception of holiness may be intimidating or fuzzy at first. But in time our minds will be renewed with the Truth, which gives us a clear perception and a reflection of God's glory."[11] Jamison names the different ways in which her own nature and her natural

129

desires hinder her efforts to embrace holiness and a fulfilling life of marriage. She concludes that holiness "goes against our flesh. It is in opposition to our natures." This natural resistance to holiness is grounded in our resistance to Jesus' holiness. To overcome this natural resistance Jamison advises the reader to "rest in Jesus." She writes, "Adore Him for yourself. . . . You will . . . find that reclaiming intimacy in your marriage is not only possible—*it is natural.*" Resting in Jesus suddenly brings to light a different experience of nature, one in which it is in line with holiness. Nature corrupted becomes nature redeemed through passivity, that is, through resting in Jesus, adoring Jesus, and trusting Jesus to fulfill our needs.[12]

What does all this mean for the production of normative Christian sexuality? In the world created by the Focus texts, the attack-queer homosexual hyper-male and the lesbian feminist represent nature corrupted by sin. More importantly, these homosexual characters represent nature refusing redemption. The gender-unstable gay and lesbian, on the other hand, represent nature redeemable. If these men and women embrace their places on the continuum of submission, then their sexual sins can be redeemed. By turning to Jesus, the feminized gay finds redemption of his nature. If this type of male homosexual actively embraces Jesus and passively "rests in Jesus," then Jesus will restore his masculinity. Likewise, Anne Paulk found the ability to acknowledge her femininity by submitting to Jesus and realizing that submission does not mean abuse.[13]

In this body theology of natural redemption we find therefore an intricate play of agency (a play not unfamiliar to students of Christian theology). On one hand, the Christian man has to rest in Jesus or submit to the power of God. On the other hand, this submission to divine power itself is an activity: "Submission means 'to submit yourself.'"[14] And as we have already seen, the ideal Christian woman has to submit to her husband and to God while resisting abuse. A tension between activity and passivity is inherent in the mode of bodily producing normative Christian sexuality. Folded into the production of an ever-unstable normative masculinity and femininity are reflections on nature and grace. None of this is made explicit. Instead of conceptual religious thought, we can glean an embodied theology from the texts of Focus on the Family. Seen through the lens of this analysis, the nearly obsessive need for the discursive production of homosexualities within the world of Focus makes sense. It is a centerpiece for the ideal of normative Christian sexuality in its (equally normative) impossibility and thus permanent mode of crisis.

AGENCIES AS CRISIS

This crisis of nature is related to a crisis of agency and to the theological conundrum of grace, that is, the question of how to negotiate the relationship between God's power and human power in the drama of salvation. In numerous systematic attempts, theologians over the centuries have tried to solve the tension between human freedom and divine agency. God's saving gift to the human soul was thought by some to be given in complete freedom and to be efficacious because of God's power alone. The divine presence in the human soul is a free favor; and so is the efficacious change of said soul through God's presence and God's favorable attitude toward the human being. However, human beings can be held responsible for their rejection of this divine offering only if they have the freedom to accept or reject it. This tension leads to the following set of questions: Is Christian redemption solely the work of divinity, and if so, is it possible that the Christian God redeems a person even against her will? Does it make a difference whether a sinner turns to God and wants to receive the gift of God's redemption, and if it does, in which sense can we say that God's saving grace is completely free? How much of the redemptive process is related to human or divine power? These questions have continued to vex Christians, and all logically possible answers have been defended and critiqued at one point or another. This is not the place to recount this tumultuous history.

However, let me remind us of what Jordan said about his own ideal marriage theology. An important function of it was "recalling as often as necessary how difficult it is to tell what divine agency might look like in erotically coupled lives."[15] In a strange turn we can read the embodied marriage theology of Focus and other producers of conservative Christian culture as doing precisely that: Their tension-filled texts, which force the reader into a spiral of constant realignments and negotiations, drive home how excruciatingly difficult it is to find out what divine or human agency might look like in the drama of the Christian life.

Indeed, already our analysis of conservative Christian attitudes toward scripture showed that it is not easy to find the right kind of distribution of agency when it comes to reading the biblical text. Submitting to the voice of the Spirit is essential so that we can stand in the gap and make present the efficacious word of God. As in the sacramental theology of the liturgical churches, human and divine actions blend in the act of reading. Yet this efficacious reading can be ratified only by those who are actively submitting themselves to the Spirit. The dance of agency finds no clear finale in the contestations of institutional certainty. The languages of eternal biblical values, scriptural authority, and natural sexuality are part of a performance of a constant struggle.

It is important to note that the dangers of this struggle are borne mostly by women. Marie Griffith describes how she was deeply touched by the outpouring of pain of Aglow women who had suffered from sexual abuse and domestic violence. Indeed, her work shows how full of pain are the stories shared by the women who participate in this conservative Christian ministry for women and by women. The prevalence of the theme of sexual abuse in the lives of the women who gather at Aglow and even more so the half-hidden stories of ongoing domestic violence show how precariously women are positioned amid the contradictions of Christian sexuality. The topic of sexual abuse in childhood and adolescence is often part of the stories Aglow women tell to show how they triumphed over a past of sin and victimization, yet current spousal domestic violence is a more shameful topic. And Griffith tells how some of the women nurture the hope that God could transform their violence-prone husbands into caring and peaceful men.[16] The tensions of Christian masculinity endanger men to become enamored with an ideal of masculine aggression, yet women risk bearing the brunt of this aggression, even while they are called to shore up their husband's virility.

Recalling our discussion of feminine submission in chapter 4, let me point out again the unequal distribution of risk involved in the tensions of Christian sexuality performed by the texts of organizations such as Focus. Here we must heed Catharine MacKinnon's warning to be critical toward the idea of negotiation.[17] What it means to be able to negotiate the tensions of Christian sexuality differs according to where we are slated on the continuum of social power. A socioeconomically disadvantaged woman or a woman of color who battles every day with racist assumptions of white respectability has few resources to "negotiate" the volatile and tension-filled performances of Christian sexuality.

Expanding on MacKinnon's observation that "gender is a social system that divides power," we can see how the complex formation of Christian sexuality works as a system that divides power.[18] The cascade of submission distributes power unequally between men and women, and the rhetoric of respectability secures claims to middle-class identity, as we saw in chapter 3. Moreover, the ability to deal with the tensions involved in Christian sexuality differs according to gender, class, and race positions. At the same time, Christian sexuality is a system whose inherent contradictions destabilize the very lines of authority it aims to establish. Christian masculinity demands embracing natural aggression *and* feminine submission to the divine "boss"; female submission requires embracing natural passivity *and* warding off abuse and reflecting spiritual power. The apparent rigidity and repetitiveness of the conservative Christian sexual discourse creates a field of narrative clashes that shapes the Christian body as a field of tensions. The individual can experience, in the struggle for ideal Christian sexuality, a bodily regime where the conflicts of sin and redemption, of nature and civilization, of power and powerlessness, and of romance and respectability are lived out.[19]

DIVINITY AS CRISIS

These ambiguities of power and submission are not limited to the human side of things. Theological language, understood in the strictest sense of the word as language about the divine, does not stabilize this tension- and violence-filled deep play of sexuality and power. Rather, God in this sexual, political, and theological imagination itself assumes the role of a cipher at once enabling and undermining the flow of power idealized by the texts of Focus.

God, who in Dobson's words is the "boss" of the universe, is imagined to wield ultimate authority. In this sense, God is the exceedingly masculine ideal. However, participating in this masculine power requires its recipient to cultivate an attitude of perfect submission. Jesus Christ, as the ideal obedient son of the Father, is the perfect example of both submission and empowerment through passivity. Given the close link between social power and biological essence that parts of conservative Christian rhetoric on sexuality assert, it is very difficult not to read sexuality back into the divine play of power and submission. The second person of the Trinity, the Son, thus exhibits perfect femininity.

The history of Christianity, which has played out every possible configuration of the relationship between divine and human power, shows us women who adopt this logic. Historian Carolyn Walker Bynum argues that medieval saints, such as Catherine of Siena, understood their culturally ascribed femininity as a perfect path to the desired imitation of Christ. His body had assumed a certain female valence in his willingness to submit to God's will. Intensifying the "female" characteristics of passivity and suffering through extreme practices of fasting and service, these women understood their bodies to be the perfect vehicle to achieve union with Christ. They thought of themselves as more capable of becoming as submissive as the Son than men, who were encumbered by pretenses of masculine power.[20] We might say that Catherine of Siena and others overfulfilled the culturally and theologically mandated sexual roles ascribed to them in their times. In so doing they claimed a form of bodily access to the divine that was more intimate than that provided for by church institutions, which were based on and which shored up masculine power. The idea of a feminine Son is therefore not without historical precedent and seems rooted in the logic of a theology that fuses sexual and theological power.

Without this link we could imagine alternative visions of sexuality. For example, Christian femininity could be thought to express perfectly the fullness of divine power that characterizes the Father. Or we could conceive of a masculinity that is shaped by perfect submission. That these alternative visions have not been realized in mainstream Christian theology shows a certain desire to sexualize as female the submissive position in conservative Christian language about power. This sexualizing equates being powerful with being masculine.

Such a move helps to support the cascade of submission that characterized the heterosexual power differences at the heart of middle-class respectability. In our analysis of the debates about the American marriage we saw that the contemporary altercations about marriage for same-sex couples were fueled by the arduous defense of these heterosexual differences. The forces of middle-class respectability were fused with a desire for sexual and theological stratifications of power. Political, sexual, and theological visions of authority and submission overlap and motivate each other. Sexual power differentials, which mediate political power gradients, are thereby anchored in a hierarchical conception of theological power.

However, the strategy of fixing these sexual hierarchies by extending the structures of respectable middle-class desire into the inner life of the Godhead leads to a dilemma. Either the characteristics of such sexuality successfully describe the inner life of the Godhead or they do not. If they do, we need to conclude that God is both male and female. If they do not, we need to conclude that divine Eros exceeds the structures of a human sexuality, which is unable to reveal anything about God. Consequently, human respectability and divine Eros are of a different kind. First, extending the structures of middle-class heterosexuality into the inner life of God requires us to assume that God is supremely male and female. Yet the idea that God is both perfectly masculine *and* perfectly feminine brings modern middle-class understandings of respectable sexuality and of divinity to the breaking point.[21] In a context where ascribing masculinity and femininity follows the rules of a zero-sum game, we have to conclude that the more masculine a person is, the less feminine he or she is. As much as an object cannot be both hot and cold, a person cannot be both male and female, according to this binary conceptualization of sexuality. Thus, a being that is both supremely masculine and supremely feminine is to be considered queer and explodes the modern idea that sexualities are characterized by binary alternatives.

We have two options if we want to avoid the claim that God is queer. We could first say that such a being is a logical impossibility and follow from this that the conclusion that God is queer shows (like a reductio ad absurdum) that human language about sexuality cannot effectively describe God. (For example, even claiming that God is of such perfection that in God opposites coincide acknowledges that binary concepts are not helpful in describing divinity.[22]) A second option would be to extend our language about respectable human sexuality in such a way that God can be said to be both perfectly masculine and perfectly feminine. Instead of stabilizing our current modes of understanding respectable sexuality, the perfection of God invites us to rethink them. Sexuality is not best thought of along the lines of a model of exclusive binary predicates such as hot–cold. It may be more apt to think of masculinity and femininity like the x- or y-axes in a Cartesian coordinate system, a model I take from Anne Fausto-Sterling.[23] In such a system, as many combinations of being both masculine and feminine would be possible as we can find combinations of the x and y coordinates. Be that as it may, it is clear that the strategy of extending middle-class stratifications into the divine leads to the surprising result that the meaning of human sexual differences is *not* anchored in the divine. Rather, talk about the binary of masculinity and femininity is *destabilized* by such an extension, which in turn produces a vision of a divinity that seems rather queer, that is, exceeding the bounds of respectable heterosexuality.

Avoiding such a vision of a gender-troubled God brings us to the second horn of the dilemma. This alternative strategy requires us to acknowledge that the structures of well-ordered middle-class desire *cannot* be extended into the inner life of the divine. Here the stratifications of an allegedly well-ordered human sexuality cannot tell us anything about the character of God's love. This failure of middle-class desires puts divinity beyond the reach of a respectably structured Eros. Thus, human desire for God will fall outside the bounds of an organization of sexuality, which supports a stable (middle-class) polity. Loving God is a form of desire incomparable to respectable and romantic Eros, a consequence drawn in traditionalist Roman Catholic theologies of the vowed religious life.[24] In short, either God is queer (because the structure of modern middle-class sexuality extends into the divine inner life), or the love for God is queer (because such a desire has to fall outside the characteristics of respectability).

A POLITICAL AND SEXUAL THEOLOGY OF CRISIS

Christian sexuality as a power-distributing and power-legitimizing system produces structures of desire and power that are riddled by contradictions and tensions. Yet this language of sexuality is deeply connected to the construction of an American middle class with its central interest in the preservation of the respectable heterosexual binary. The defense of this binary lies at the heart of the current defense of marriage debates, as we have seen.

Ideas about the character of God's love and power, the allegedly natural sexuality and aggression of men, the receptivity of the ideal Christian and the trope of female submission, the defense of heterosexuality from the onslaught of sexual couplings of ill repute, and the concern for the character of middle-class America: The languages used to discuss these topics all support each other. Meaning derived in one context informs the understanding of words in another. What makes conservative Christian rhetoric about same-sex love so effective in America is the fact that it resonates over the registers of theology, sexuality, and politics.

Therefore I am not convinced that conservative Christians hold onto the rhetoric of submission and to their rejection of same-sex love because they want to be countercultural. Yes, the claim that the American family is threatened "by the forces of hell," which are exemplified by the cultural actors pushing for the "homosexual agenda," is important for the self-representation of conservative Christian groups. And it is true that Christian identity seems imagined as living on the frontiers battling a dangerous culture that has forgotten what the real America is about. However, we also have seen that both in their everyday sexual arrangements and in the theory of conservative Christian sexuality, these Christians search for a balance of aggression and passivity. Far from delineating a clear countercultural boundary, Christian sexuality (in word and deed) reflects an embodied struggle in dealing with issues of male violence, dominance, and release of power. Although they live their sexual lives like other ordinary middle-class people, they speak and embody perhaps more self-consciously than some of their fellow citizens the perils of the American Eros. These Christians are not countercultural because they promote a patriarchal sexual regime; they are perhaps countercultural because they incessantly speak about it. In emphasizing the masculine nature of an aggressive sexuality and in rooting it in masculine images of the divine, conservative Christian organizations seem rather in tune with dominant understandings of sexuality.[25] Consider, for example, Catharine MacKinnon's discussion of the structures of sexual hierarchization and pornography.

> Gender and sexuality . . . become two different shapes taken by the single social equation of male with dominance and female with submission. Feeling this as identity, acting it as role, inhabiting and presenting it as self, is

the domain of gender. Enjoying it as the erotic, centering upon when it elicits genital arousal, is the domain of sexuality. Inequality is what is sexualized through pornography; it is what is sexual about it. The more unequal, the more sexual.[26]

MacKinnon correctly notes that removing the male (or the female) body from the sexual act does not undermine the matrix of power and submission. A dominatrix or a gay man who cannot find himself aroused by the body of an "effeminate" man only reinforces the definition of dominance as masculine and passivity as the nonmasculine other, the feminine. The following examples can show how widespread are these ideas in American culture.

In *Men's Lives*, Michael Kimmel and Michael A. Messner show the link between ideals of toughness, strength, and authority in American cultural constructions of dominant masculinity. "Composer Charles Ives, debunking 'sissy' types of music . . . said [that] he used traditional tough guy themes and concerns in his drive to build new sounds. . . . Or architect Louis Sullivan [describes] his ambition to create 'masculine forms': strong, solid, commanding respect."[27] Women in this vision of sexuality are not strong, lack solidity, and certainly do not command respect. Social power and authority is something that women must earn by pleasing those who wield it. Consider a scandal at Milton Academy, a prep school in New England, where, as came to light in 2005, numerous boys could command the sexual favors of girls who would fellate them in exchange for social standing. Reviewing a report on these incidents, Touré writes, "It almost always involves subservience from the girl and unequal activity, as if sex were something girls give and boys receive. 'Hooking up with guys was so rarely about her own pleasure,' the authors write of one girl. 'The acts were part of an implied social exchange: oral sex for social clout.'"[28] The leaders of Focus on the Family would clearly denounce the occurrences at Milton as sinful and hurtful to the young women involved. They might say that promiscuity, sexual activity outside marriage, the lack of respect for the purity of the women at Milton—all these are indicators of modern sexual depravity. Yet the Milton case reenacts the very structure of sexual power that Focus idealizes. Social power and sexual initiative is the realm of men, and women can find standing only by assuming their subservient role in the hierarchy of submission.

I mention this case to point out that in the symbolic universe in which Americans grow up to struggle for their sexual self-understanding, the difference between the powerful male body and the weak female body still represents how things should be. Consider the example of the cultural institution of American sports as one field where sexual identities are learned and performed. As one young white professional spectator (who admitted he was unable to perform on the football field) enthused, "A woman can do the same job as I can do—maybe even be my boss. But I'll be *damned* if she can go out on the football field and take a hit from Ronnie Lott," who epitomized for him the fear-inspiring football player.[29] Newscasters extol the "heroes," "gladiators," "top guns," or "warriors" of American sports with the language of military conquest, violence, and destruction. Importantly, here American masculinity is imagined not only as a realization of "natural" dominance over women but also as a field of permanent competition between men, and this fact makes the field of sports particularly interesting for our inquiry. The battle of America's gladiators for dominance on the field is presented as a combat over claims to superior masculinity. The losers are sissies, not men enough, "girly men" in the infamous words of Arnold Schwarzenegger. They are like women. The winners realize their position on top of the hierarchy of submission.

We saw how the hypo-male gay made visible in the world of Focus the fear that a man may lose his masculinity or may not be manly enough, lacking the necessary roughness and aggression. In fact, Dr. Dobson's psychological advice for "gender disturbed" children aimed to shore up a boy's "natural" aggression or assure a girl in her "natural" passivity. This understanding of masculinity is not at all countercultural. Rather, ideal Christian sexuality, as it appears in the texts of Focus, is linked to other cultural practices that perform American manhood. The young reader of, say *Breakaway*, is invited not only to internalize the image of a powerful God ("the boss") or to follow the advice on Christian sexuality but also to engage in the workout regimen that the magazine offers; and he will hear in the texts of Focus echoes of the messages about what makes an American man, which are broadcast as part of his radio's football coverage.

At the same time, it is important to note that masculine power is neither uniformly produced nor equally accessible to all males. "Because different masculinities are ordered in a hierarchy, different white, black, or working-class men will experience power differently and will have different access, socially and economically, to ways of accruing power and to the institutions of power," writes sociologist Anne Cossins.[30] Thus masculinity is produced not only through the contrast with femininity. What constitutes masculine power is also the result of racial and class boundaries. American masculinities are therefore the result of contrasts gained through the hierarchizing ideas of race and class as well. Part of the production of white masculinity, for example, is the imagination and cultural depiction of black male sexuality as out of bounds, violent, and savage.[31] This cultural imagination has deep roots in the legitimization of European and American colonial violence. Native men were presented as being overly feminine or childlike (and thus needing European masculine rule) or as overly violent and masculine (hence threatening the European family and their women).[32] In contrast to this sexuality out of bounds, white colonial or white middle-class sexuality is characterized by civilized restraint. We have seen a similar unbounded male body, namely that of the oversexed hyper-male attack-gay, in Focus on the Family texts. This deviant gay body functions in analogy to the construction of the "savage black male," namely to stabilize respectable middle-class masculinity. While the gladiators of the football field capture the attention of the professional male spectator, only civilized restraint will turn them into potential husbands for the daughters of good middle-class families.

In sum, Focus's strategy of defining normative American masculinity by rejecting the "effeminized" gay and by simultaneously containing allegedly natural and dangerous male aggression is not at all countercultural. Rather, this strategy is deeply connected to middle-class visions of how to produce (white, respectable) masculine power. Respectable middle-class masculinity occupies a central role in the American polity, as scholar of masculinities Michael Kimmel writes:

> One definition of manhood continues to remain the standard against which other forms of manhood are measured and evaluated. Within the dominant culture, the masculinity that defines white, middle class, early middle-aged

heterosexual men is the masculinity that sets the standards for other men, against which other men are measured and, more often than not, found wanting.[33]

Therefore, conservative Christian language about same-sex love connects with and reinforces the shaping of middle-class sexualities in their normative distribution of power. The narrative inventions of the feminist lesbian, the gender-disturbed gay, or his oversexed counterpart and the painful reminders of the lives of abused women function like the arena of American sports: They present a deep play where spectators and actors alike can get lost in performing with overdrawn clarity the tensions of the American sexual regime.[34] Here it is made clear what makes men into men and women into women; here it is where the impossibilities of American and Christian sexualities are lived out.

In her magisterial work on American marriage, Nancy Cott concludes that sexuality is not disestablished in the contemporary United States. With this phrase she means to point out that the state still sees it as a legitimate and necessary task to regulate how American citizens live their sexual lives. Like a regime of established churches that allows only certain modes of living one's religious life, the federal government and many state governments sanction only certain limited versions of forming a sexual partnership. This is the publicly recognized form of heterosexual marriage, which is defended with the help of the rhetorical invention of an unchangeable Christian marriage tradition.[35]

Our inquiry allows us to extend Cott's formulation. As defenders of the middle-class vision of what characterizes the nation, the United States government and the individual states have an interest in enabling the deep play of heterosexual power differentials. What keeps the nation at play are the tensions between inclusive romance and stratifying respectability, between authority and submission, between idealized masculine power and feminine passivity, between human power and divine agency, and between God and Eros.

NOTES

1.   Greenberg, *Wrestling with God and Men*; Jordan, *Blessing Same-Sex Unions*; Rogers, *Sexuality and the Christian Body*; Viefhues, " 'On My Bed at Night I Sought Him Whom My Heart Loves.' "

I. INTRODUCTION

1.   For a description of the religious roots of gay and lesbian liberation, see Jordan, *Blessing Same-Sex Unions*. For the changes in American attitudes toward gays and lesbians, see the opening of Chauncey, *Why Marriage?*

2.   My analysis will explain why in the United States marital relationships are *not* disestablished, to use a phrase Nancy Cott coins to point out that the U.S. federal and state governments consider it to be in their legitimate interests to regulate the sexual practices of Americans. Moreover, I will demonstrate in detail how religious language is successfully used in the creation of state-sanctioned respectable sexuality. Janet Jakobsen and Anne Pellegrini's call to disestablish sexuality (and religion) appears to be both well taken and overly optimistic. Based on an examination of the specific character of particular conservative Christian languages about sexuality and power, I will

show that the interplay of middle-class sexual and conservative Christian religious values is ingrained deeply in the formation of the American nation. Unlike that of Jakobsen and Pellegrini, my analysis traces this religious and sexual interaction into the heart of the formation of modern middle-class subjectivity (chapter 3) and political power in the nation-state. By making their project more specific, my analysis shows how utopian it is to demand a disestablished sexuality in the modern nation-state. Thus Cott's more sanguine conclusion reflects a necessity of modern sexual and religious politics. Cott, *Public Vows*, 212; Jakobsen and Pellegrini, *Love the Sin*.

3. Wuthnow, *The Restructuring of American Religion*. I also follow Benedict Anderson in his interest in the shaping of the nation as imagined community. Anderson, *Imagined Communities*.

4. Jordan, *Blessing Same-Sex Unions*, 120.

5. Cf. Greeley and Hout, *The Truth About Conservative Christians*, 3.

6. Shea, *The Lion and the Lamb*. Quoted in Greeley and Hout, *The Truth About Conservative Christians*, 13.

7. Bebbington, *Evangelicalism in Modern Britain*.

8. Alan Wolfe, "Response."

9. For the idea that a religious tradition consists of those claimed by a text (or a history of texts), see Plaskow, *Standing Again at Sinai*.

10. Catholic Church, *Catechism*, n.107.

11. See Greeley and Hout, *The Truth About Conservative Christians*, 6.

12. Toalston, "Amid a Culture That Has Left Many Families Frayed and Others Battered."

13. Apostolidis, *Stations of the Cross*.

14. Cf. Hendershot, *Shaking the World for Jesus*, 89.

15. Ibid. Also, cf. Hunter, *American Evangelicalism*, 99.

16. Hendershot, *Shaking the World for Jesus*, 88; Diamond, *Not by Politics Alone*, 31.

17. Gallagher, *Evangelical Identity*, 172.

18. Diamond, *Not by Politics Alone*, 32.

19. Connolly, "The Evangelical-Capitalist Resonance Machine."

20. Cf. Griffith, *God's Daughters*, 18.

21. Wolfe, "Response," 106.

22. Wolfe, "The Culture War That Never Came."

23. Glaeser and Ward, *Myths and Realities of American Political Geography*, 31, 33.

24. Brown, *Other Voices, Other Worlds*; Rogers, *Sexuality and the Christian Body*.

25. See Johnson, *A Time to Embrace*. Although this work discusses the issue under the rubrics of religion, law, and politics, Johnson does not analyze religious claims as being formed under the influences of this triad.

26. Gallagher, *Evangelical Identity*; Greeley and Hout, *The Truth About Conservative Christians*; Griffith, *God's Daughters*; Moon, *God, Sex, and Politics*; Smith, *Christian America?*

27. Phillips, *American Theocracy*.

28. Unfortunately, Cobb's analysis of religious rhetoric on the issue of same-sex love reiterates the vision of a single language of Christian sovereignty. Incidentally, we will see that the religious language circulated among conservative Christians is similar to the literary examples he cites in its paradoxical and conflicted nature. Cobb, *God Hates Fags*.

29. Orsi, *The Madonna of 115th Street*; Hannerz, *Cultural Complexity*.

30. Jakobsen and Pellegrini, *Love the Sin*, 13. The trouble with this otherwise very incisive book is that the authors do not differentiate in their analyses between different Christian discourses about same-sex love but talk about "Protestantism" in the singular as shaping the nation's moral ideals (p. 22). In so doing they reproduce the image of a monolithic conservative Christianity, which numerous recent anthropological studies in the vein of Gallagher and Smith have undermined.

31. Gallup Europe, EOS. "Public Opinion and Same-Sex Unions."

32. Gallagher, *Evangelical Identity* and "Where Are the Antifeminist Evangelicals?"

33. Gallagher, *Evangelical Identity*, 83.

34. Roy, *Globalized Islam*.

35. Eisenstadt, "The Transformations of the Religious Dimensions in the Constitution of Contemporary Modernities."

36. Eickelman and Piscatory coined the concept of "objectified Islam" in Eickelman and Piscatory, *Muslim Politics*. This notion differs from De Certeau's idea of "objective Christianity" as the institution connecting individual experience with society. Certeau and Domenach, *Le Christianisme Eclate*.

37. Wolfe, "Response," 101.

38. Roy, *Globalized Islam*.

39. Smith, *Christian America?*, 191.

40. Harding, "Convicted by the Holy Spirit."

41. Harding, "Convicted by the Holy Spirit," 167; cf. Griffith, *God's Daughters*, 202.

42. Pew Research Center for the People and the Press, *Religious Beliefs Underpin Opposition to Homosexuality.*

43. For the idea of shortcuts, cf. Posner, *Law, Pragmatism, and Democracy*, 144.

44. Hunter, "The Enduring Culture War," 33.

45. Holsinger, *Pathophysiology of Male Homosexuality.*

46. Here my project aligns with that of Jakobsen and Pellegrini, who write that "attention to how homosexuality is talked about and represented in any number of public venues allows us to glimpse larger processes of American national identity formation and thereby to ask some difficult questions: How are the contours of American belonging shaped and reshaped? What public language is available for talking about what we value and why? And just who are the 'we' who talk and talk some more?" Jakobsen and Pellegrini, *Love the Sin*, 15.

47. Viefhues-Bailey, *Beyond the Philosopher's Fear*, 55–62.

48. In a fully private language, the words that describe this fleeting sensation have to be comprehensively defined by it. For example, let the meaning of the artificial private word *blub* be defined by the sensation S at T1. If that is the case, this word cannot describe the later sensation S at T2, because *blub* is by definition S at T1. Technically speaking: because its definition is exclusively tied to a specific context, *blub* functions not like a concept but like a singular term. The situation is different if *blub* is my private codeword for *joy*. Here the meaning of *blub* is established by the publicly negotiated meaning of *joy*. Given this publicly established meaning I can decide whether S at T2 can count as being *blub*.

49. Viefhues-Bailey, *Beyond the Philosopher's Fear*, chapters 2 and 3.

50. The contrast here is a Bourdieuian idea of practice: Bourdieu, *Outline of a Theory of Practice*, 5–6, 163–164.

51. "When we first begin to *believe* anything, what we believe is not a single proposition, it is a whole system of propositions. (Light dawns gradually over the whole)." Wittgenstein et al., *On Certainty*, §141.

52. Wittgenstein and Anscombe, *Philosophical Investigations*, §121.

53. His most famous example is that of the word *game*. By thinking about all the different things and activities we call games, we can explore the extension of what *we* mean by *game*. "Isn't my knowledge, my concept of a game, completely expressed in the explanations that I could give? That is, in my describing examples of various kinds of game; showing how all sorts of other games can be constructed on the analogy of these; say that I should scarcely include

this or this among games; and so on." Wittgenstein and Anscombe, *Philosophical Investigations*, §75.

54. Jäger, "Diskurs und Wissen," 83.

55. See Phillips, *Faith and Philosophical Enquiry*.

56. Wittgenstein et al., *On Certainty*, §143.

57. Wolfe, "The Culture War That Never Came," 48. Examples of how gay Evangelicals negotiate their sexual and religious identity can be found in Thurma, "Negotiating a Religious Identity."

2. RELIGIOUS INTERESTS BETWEEN BIBLE AND POLITICS

1. Gallagher, *Evangelical Identity*, 79.

2. Wolfe, "Response," 106.

3. Bartkowski, *Remaking the Godly Marriage*; Gallagher, *Evangelical Identity*; Griffith, *God's Daughters*; Smith, *Christian America?*

4. Bartkowski, *Remaking the Godly Marriage*, 164; Gallagher, *Evangelical Identity*, 77. Studies such as these paint a more life-size picture of Evangelical Christianity than even James Hunter's seminal *Culture Wars* or Phillips's more anxious *American Theocracy*.

5. Smith, *Christian America?*, 215.

6. Bartkowski, *Remaking the Godly Marriage*, 163; Gallagher, *Evangelical Identity*, 79ff.

7. Soulforce (see http://www.soulforce.org). For a critical analysis of this organization's indebtedness to Evangelical constructions of sexual orientation, see Chavez, "Beyond Complicity."

8. See Moon, *God, Sex, and Politics*, 57–58.

9. Smith, *Christian America?*, 225.

10. Herman, *The Antigay Agenda*, 12.

11. Ross, "Hey Mike."

12. Watters, "BA: Silent in Church."

13. Article 2 of the Lausanne covenant reprinted in: Gallagher, *Evangelical Identity*, 78. Inerrancy was a position developed in the late nineteenth century by professors at Princeton seminary in reaction to German-style biblical criticism. This European school of scriptural interpretation studied the historical development of the biblical texts, tried to find the earliest textual strata, and discussed the multiple differences between them. Instead of a unified biblical

147

text, this method presented a patchwork of texts and recensions. The 1974 meeting was convened by a committee chaired by Billy Graham and was attended by representatives from more than 150 countries. The text of the covenant can be found at http://www.lausanne.org/lausanne-1974/lausanne-1974.html.

14. Harding, *The Book of Jerry Falwell*, 28.

15. The image of standing in the gap is taken from Ezekiel 22:30, and its deployment is itself an example of the creativity of biblical interpretation. Cf. Harding, *The Book of Jerry Falwell*, 12.

16. Harding, *The Book of Jerry Falwell*, 46.

17. McGinn, *The Growth of Mysticism*, 331.

18. Gallagher, "Where Are the Antifeminist Evangelicals?," 172.

19. Harding, *The Book of Jerry Falwell*, 26.

20. Ibid.

21. Ibid., 28, 25.

22. Dailey, "Sex, Segregation, and the Sacred After *Brown*."

23. Harding, *The Book of Jerry Falwell*, 180ff.

24. Pew Research Center for the People and the Press, *Religious Beliefs Underpin Opposition to Homosexuality*.

25. Gallagher, *Evangelical Identity*, 82, and "Where Are the Antifeminist Evangelicals?"

26. Eco, *Six Walks in the Fictional Woods*, 83.

27. Frank, *What Is the Matter with Kansas?*

28. Wolfe, "The Culture War That Never Came," 54.

29. Ibid.

30. Pew Research Center for the People and the Press, *Religious Beliefs Underpin Opposition to Homosexuality*, 14.

31. Smith, *Christian America?*, 208.

32. Hunter, "The Enduring Culture War."

33. Ibid., 14, 15.

34. Ibid., 26.

35. Wolfe, "The Culture War That Never Came," 49.

36. He traces his position back to a structuralism in sociology originating with Durkheim, Luhmann, and Douglas. Wolfe, "Response," 99.

37. Bakhtin and Holquist, *The Dialogic Imagination*, 293–294. Bakhtin is a particularly interesting figure because the Russian literary theorist had to deal with attempts by the Soviet government to regulate and shape officially acceptable

language. This was an extreme case of powerful elites trying to impose standards of appropriate speech. Thus, we can see in his work both an acknowledgment of the power of elites to shape language and a realization of the limitations of this power. Yet acknowledging limitations does not mean that everyone is equal when it comes using speech. Cf. Smith, *Language and Power*.

38. Harding, *The Book of Jerry Falwell*, 58.

39. Griffith, *God's Daughters*, 200.

40. Anthropologist Michel de Certeau calls this the ideology of "'informing' through books." Certeau, *The Practice of Everyday Life*, 166.

41. Hunter, "The Enduring Culture War," 90–101.

42. Wolfe, "Response," 101–102.

43. Wolfe, "The Culture War That Never Came," 63.

44. Wolfe, "Response," 106.

45. Gallagher, *Evangelical Identity*, 172.

46. Focus on the Family, *Husbands and Wives: Homosexuality*.

47. Marx, *The Eighteenth Brumaire*, 15.

48. Utvik, "The Modernizing Force of Islam," 66.

49. Tambiah, *Buddhism Betrayed?*, 118.

50. Ibid., 20.

51. Hallisey, "Roads Taken and Not Taken."

52. Wolfe, "Response," 103.

53. Chatterjee, *The Nation and Its Fragments*.

54. Ibid., 104, 145.

55. Ibid., 126.

56. Ibid., 131.

57. Tambiah, *Buddhism Betrayed?*, 12.

58. Oakeshott and Fuller, *Religion, Politics, and the Moral Life*.

59. Cf. Roy, *Globalized Islam*, 166.

149

3. AMERICA AND THE STATE OF RESPECTABLE CHRISTIAN ROMANCE

1. Sprigg, "Questions and Answers."

2. Ibid.

3. "The Gay Marriage Debate."

4. Stanton, "What's the Deal with Same-Sex Marriage?"

5. Ibid.

6. Stanton, "Is Marriage in Jeopardy?" Incidentally, this material was used in the campaigning for Proposition 8 in California, which in the fall of 2008 restricted marriage to heterosexual couples.

7. Sprigg and Dailey, *Getting It Straight*.

8. Stanton, "What's the Deal with Same-Sex Marriage?"

9. Sprigg, *Questions and Answers*.

10. Ibid.

11. Echols, "Cultural Feminism," 47.

12. United States Congress, "Congressional Record—House" (1996), p. H7493.

13. United States Congress, "Congressional Record—Senate" (1996b), p. S10109.

14. United States Congress, "Congressional Record—Senate" (1996a), p. S10068.

15. Jordan, *Blessing Same-Sex Unions*, 100.

16. Shellenberger, "Heaven."

17. Jordan, *Blessing Same-Sex Unions*, 160ff.

18. Thomas Aquinas, *Scriptum in Sentenciis*, 4.33.1.1 corpus, responses 1 & 2, and 4.33.1.2 corpus and responses to the counterarguments, as cited in Jordan, *Blessing Same-Sex Unions*, 161, 163.

19. Jordan, *Blessing Same-Sex Unions*, 164.

20. Jordan, *Ethics of Sex*, 74.

21. Jordan, *Blessing Same-Sex Unions*, 120.

22. Ibid.

23. Ibid., 24.

24. Ibid., 8.

25. Ibid., 24.

26. Dobson, "Dr. Dobson's Study, Excerpts from Complete Marriage and Family Home Reference Guide," 2002.

27. Cott, *Public Vows*, 4.

28. Ibid., 113.

29. Lieber, "The Mormons," 234. Quoted in Cott, *Public Vows*, 115.

30. Cott, *Public Vows*, 116.

31. Cott, *Public Vows*, 131.

32. *Reynolds v. United States*. Supreme Court of the United States 98 U.S. 145 October, 1878, Term.

33. Stoler, *Carnal Knowledge*, 150. This discussion is clearly indebted to Foucault's idea of biopolitics. Foucault, *"Il Faut Défendre la Société."*

34. Cott, *Public Vows*, 144f, 155.

35. Ibid., 10.

36. Lynd and Lynd, *Middletown*, 114ff. Cott, *Public Vows*, 150.

37. Cavell, *Pursuit of Happiness*, 31.

38. Dobson, *Bringing Up Boys*, 118.

39. For Cavell's political philosophy, see Viefhues-Bailey, *Beyond the Philosopher's Fear*.

40. Mosse, *Nationalism and Sexuality*.

41. Cott, *Public Vows*, 20.

42. Cott, *Public Vows*, 20, 17.

43. Consider what Stoler writes about the situation in colonial Java: "European children of the well-to-do were at risk if the proper habitus was not assured, if socializing with poor children of mixed parentage was not monitored and certain social protocols were not met. The risk . . . was that their sense of 'belonging' and their longings allowed in too much that was locally acquired and Javanese." Stoler, *Carnal Knowledge*, 153.

44. Higginbotham, *Righteous Discontent*, 14ff, 188. Also see Carby, "The Multicultural Wars"; and Davey, "Outing Whiteness."

45. *Jay Brause and Gene Dugan v. Bureau of Vital Statistics, Alaska* (Superior Court for the State of Alaska, 3d. Jud District. Peter Michalski Judge, 2/27/1998). Quoted in Cott, *Public Vows*, 216.

46. Jordan, *Blessing Same-Sex Unions*, 38.

47. Cott, *Public Vows*, 225

48. Jordan, *Blessing Same-Sex Unions*, 45.

49. Ibid., 25.

50. Dobson, *Marriage Under Fire*, 49.

51. Jordan, "Excerpt from Santorum Interview." For Talent, see Cott, *Public Vows*, 219.

52. Dobson, "In Defending Marriage—Take the Offensive."

53. Congressional Record at H7491 (daily ed. 12th July, 1996) (statement of Rep. Canady). Quoted in Feldblum, "The Limitations of Liberal Neutrality Arguments," 67.

54. Cott, *Public Vows*, 220.

55. Pew Research Center for the People and the Press, *Religious Beliefs Underpin Opposition to Homosexuality*, 7.

56. Cott and Chauncey seem to assume that this is the issue. Cott, *Public Vows*, 221; Chauncey, *Why Marriage?*, 163ff.

57. Cott, *Public Vows*, 212.

58. Gallagher, *Evangelical Identity*, 172.

59. Nagel, "Masculinity and Nationalism," 122. See also McClintock, *Imperial Leather*.

4. SAME-SEX LOVE AND THE IMPOSSIBILITY OF CHRISTIAN FEMININITY AND MASCULINITY

1. Dobson, *Complete Marriage and Family Home Reference Guide*, 416. Also see Dobson, "Dr. Dobson's Study, Excerpts from *Complete Marriage and Family Home Reference Guide*, Stable Society."

2. Smith, *Christian America?*, 212, 217, 225.

3. Dobson, "Dr. Dobson's Study, Excerpts from *Complete Marriage and Family Home Reference Guide*, Letter to a Gay Man."

4. Pew Research Center for the People and the Press, *Religious Beliefs Underpin Opposition to Homosexuality*.

5. Greenhouse, "The Supreme Court."

6. Herman, *The Antigay Agenda*, 78.

7. Focus on the Family, *Husbands & Wives: Homosexuality*.

8. Dobson, "Dr. Dobson's Study, February 2000."

9. Harvey, *A Checklist to Assess Your School's Risk for Encouraging Homosexuality*.

10. Nicolosi, *Is This Really Good for Kids?*

11. Dobson, *Complete Marriage and Family Home Reference Guide*, 402; Dobson, *Troubled With: Homosexuality*.

12. Kaufman, *Not Afraid to Come Out*.

13. Kaufman, *Gay Culture 101*.

14. Dobson, *Bringing Up Boys*, 124–125.

15. Swift, "The Gay Manifesto."

16. Ibid.

17. Dobson, *Bringing Up Boys*, 125–126.

18. Kaufman, *Not Afraid to Come Out*.

19. Dobson, "Dr. Dobson's Study, November, 1998."

20. Dobson, *Complete Marriage and Family Home Reference Guide*, 410.

21. Dobson, "Dr. Dobson's Study, Excerpts from *Complete Marriage and Family Home Reference Guide*, Letter to a Gay Man."

22. Jordahl, *New Hate Crime Stats Released*.

23. Dobson, *Bringing Up Boys*, 2, 4, 27.

24. Ross, "Hey Mike: Don't Be Controlled by Lust."

25. Shellenberger, "Dear Susi: Privacy and Dealing with Guys."

26. These findings echo Didi Herman's readings of anti–gay and lesbian rhetoric in the Christian Right in general. According to Herman, gay desires embody for the Christian Right a "hyper-masculinity, a maleness so extreme it literally (ex)implodes." Herman, *The Antigay Agenda*, 81ff.

27. This letter talks about how the boy tried to "suck [his] own penis," lusts at himself "wearing skimpy underwear," and enjoys the "sexual sensation" when he wiggles his "body rapidly, making [his] genitals bounce up and down." The reader wonders why Dobson circulates this piece in detail. James Dobson, "Dr. Dobson's Study, June 2002."

28. Dobson, *Bringing Up Boys*, 118.

29. Nicolosi as quoted in Dobson, *Bringing Up Boys*, 118, 122.

30. Paulk and Paulk, "The Other Way Out." Stonewall Revisited hosts a number of "coming out of homosexuality" stories. Another example is Alan's story: "In my background were most of the ingredients typically seen as contributing to homosexuality: an unplanned child, parents who were hoping for a girl, an older brother who met the father's ideal more than I, and a father with severe emotional problems which caused him to barely be able to cope with life himself, much less meet the needs of his son." Mendinger, "He Healed My Marriage."

31. Paulk, "Former Lesbian."

32. Dobson, "To the Husbands of Christian Homemakers." (2002) available from http://web.archive.org/web/20020307012938/http://www.family.org/married/comm/a0019596.cfm.13.

33. Comiskey, How Jesus Heals Us Through His Church. Also see Citizenlink, "Help for the Homosexual."

34. Dobson, "Dr. Dobson's Study, June 1998."

35. Koerner, "The Temptation to Fudge."

36. Hendershot, *Shaking the World for Jesus*, 93.

37. Herman, *The Antigay Agenda*, 98ff, 104, 107.

38. Ryan, "Please Open My Door."

39. Bartkowski, *Remaking the Godly Marriage*, 59.

40. Kroeger and Nason-Clark, *No Place for Abuse*. Cf. Gallagher, *Evangelical Identity*, 166.

41. Stewart, "Signs of an Abusive Relationship."

153

42. Bartkowski, *Remaking the Godly Marriage*, 41; Dobson, *What Wives Wish*.

43. As quoted by Bartkowski, *Remaking the Godly Marriage*, 41. LaHaye, *The Spirit Controlled Woman*, 41.

44. Ryan, "Please Open My Door."

45. Rae, "Does Christianity Support the Oppression of Women?" (Rae, a missionary, repeats the trope of contrasting the violently oppressed heathen woman with the well-cared-for Christian American woman.)

46. Ryan, "Please Open My Door."

47. Rae, "Does Christianity Support the Oppression of Women?"

48. Cooper, *You Can Be the Wife of a Happy Husband*, 66. As quoted in Bartkowski, *Remaking the Godly Marriage*, 56 (italics added).

49. Rae, "Does Christianity Support the Oppression of Women?"

50. Ibid.

51. Gallagher, *Evangelical Identity*, 165.

52. Ibid., 94.

53. Griffith, *God's Daughters*, 103.

54. Ibid., 155.

55. Bartkowski, *Remaking the Godly Marriage*, 120.

56. Griffith, *God's Daughters*, 180.

57. Ibid., 181.

58. Gallagher, *Evangelical Identity*, 165; Groothuis, *Good News for Women*, 54.

59. Gallagher, *Evangelical Identity*, 116.

60. Ibid., 149.

61. Ibid., 104.

62. Ryan, "Please Open My Door."

5. A POLITICAL AND SEXUAL THEOLOGY OF CRISIS

1. Gallagher, *Evangelical Identity*, 173; Smith, *Christian America?*, 191.

2. Gallagher, *Evangelical Identity*, 84.

3. Bartkowski, *Remaking the Godly Marriage*, 40.

4. James Dobson, *Bringing Up Boys*, 26–27, 122.

5. Ibid.

6. Dobson, *Straight Talk*, 132. As quoted in Bartkowski, *Remaking the Godly Marriage*, 45.

7. Hendershot finds a similar tension in abstinence discourse. Hendershot, *Shaking the World for Jesus*, 92ff.

8. Butler, *Bodies That Matter*, 1.

9. Ibid., 1–2.

10. Dobson, "To the Husbands of Christian Homemakers."

11. Jamison, "Pursuing Holiness in Marriage."

12. Ibid., ¶11, ¶25, ¶26 (italics added).

13. This complex play of agency, both sexual and religious, is not peculiar to Evangelical Christianity. See Clark, *Where Men Are Wives*.

14. Stormie Omartian, "How Husbands Handle Submission."

15. Jordan, *Blessing Same-Sex Unions*, 120.

16. Griffith, *God's Daughters*, 4, 113, 116.

17. MacKinnon, *Toward a Feminist Theory of the State*.

18. Ibid.

19. This position seems similar what Cobb describes in his literary analysis of the religious language used by the character Celie in Alice Walker's *The Color Purple*. "Walker has Celie learn to write to her sister . . . offering the possibility of a sinister and terrible formulation of the representation and recognition . . . of sexuality that is nevertheless an ambiguous language of God—a language that is strangely productive of unimaginable pleasure and connection." Cobb, *God Hates Fags*, 171.

20. Bynum, *Holy Feast and Holy Fast*.

21. For a historical and systematic critique of the modern system of organizing sexuality, see Fausto-Sterling, *Sexing the Body*; Laqueur, *Making Sex*.

22. Analogical predication obscures more than it reveals: God is hot(A) and God is cold(A), where (A) indicates a binary predicate of such a nature that both the predicate and its opposite can be predicated. In other words, the hotness of God is special because it admits for the simultaneous presence of a special kind of coldness, which admits for the presence of the special kind of hotness. Instead of learning what God is, we learn more about the limits of our language. Be that as it may, by definition the predicate hot(A) differs from the predicate hot, used for ordinary objects.

23. Fausto-Sterling, *Sexing the Body*, chapter 9.

24. For a contemporary version of such theologies, see Viefhues, "'On My Bed at Night I Sought Him Whom My Heart Loves.'"

25. For the widespread understanding of adolescent male sexuality as aggressive, see Pollack, *Real Boys*.

26. MacKinnon, *Toward a Feminist Theory of the State*, 143.

27. Kimmel and Messner, *Men's Lives*, xiii. See also Cossins, *Masculinities*, 95.

28. Touré, "Dirty Pretty Things." (Note the rather sexist title of Touré's review).

29. Messner, "Masculinities and Athletic Careers," 67. See also Cossins, *Masculinities*, 95.

30. Cossins, *Masculinities*, 106.

31. Giroux, "Racial Politics and the Pedagogy of Whiteness," 295.

32. For one of many examples of this rhetoric, see Stoler, *Carnal Knowledge*.

33. Kimmel, "Masculinity as Homophobia," 124–125.

34. Deep play is a notion successfully used by Geertz, *Interpretation of Cultures*.

35. Cott, *Public Vows*, 212.

BIBLIOGRAPHY

Anderson, Benedict. *Imagined communities: Reflections on the origin and spread of*   157
   nationalism. London: Verso, 1983.

Apostolidis, Paul. *Stations of the Cross: Adorno and Christian right radio.* Durham:
   Duke University Press, 2000.

Bakhtin, M. M. and Michael Holquist. *The dialogic imagination: Four essays.* University of Texas Press Slavic Series, no. 1. Austin: University of Texas Press,
   1981.

Bartkowski, John P. *Remaking the godly marriage: Gender negotiation in Evangelical*
   families. New Brunswick, N.J.: Rutgers University Press, 2001.

Bebbington, D. W. *Evangelicalism in modern Britain: A history from the 1730s to the*
   1980s. London: Unwin Hyman, 1989.

Bourdieu, Pierre. *Outline of a theory of practice.* Cambridge Studies in Social Anthropology, no. 16. Cambridge: Cambridge University Press, 1977.

Brown, Terry. *Other voices, other worlds: The global church speaks out on homosexual-*
   ity. London: Darton Longman and Todd, 2006.

Butler, Judith. *Bodies that matter: On the discursive limits of "sex."* New York: Routledge, 1993.

Bynum, Caroline Walker. *Holy feast and holy fast: The religious significance of food to*
   medieval women. Berkeley: University of California Press, 1987.

Carby, Hazel V. The multicultural wars. In *Black popular culture: A project*, ed. Michele Wallace and Gina Dent, 187–199. Seattle: Bay Press, 1992.

Catholic Church. *Catechism of the Catholic Church*. Chicago: Loyola University Press; Vatican City: Libreria Editrice Vaticana, 1994.

Cavell, Stanley. *Pursuits of happiness: The Hollywood comedy of remarriage*. Harvard Film Studies. Cambridge, Mass.: Harvard University Press, 1981.

Certeau, Michel de. *The practice of everyday life*. Berkeley: University of California Press, 1984.

Certeau, Michel de and Jean-Marie Domenach. *Le christianisme eclate*. Paris: Edition du Seuil, 1974.

Chatterjee, Partha. *The nation and its fragments: Colonial and postcolonial histories*. Princeton Studies in Culture/Power/History. Princeton, N.J.: Princeton University Press, 1993.

Chauncey, George. *Why marriage? The history shaping today's debate over gay equality*. Cambridge, Mass.: Basic Books, 2004.

Chavez, Karma R. Beyond complicity: Coherence, queer theory, and the rhetoric of the "gay Christian movement." *Text and Performance Quarterly* 24, no. 3/4 (2004): 255–275.

Citizenlink. Help for the homosexual. Focus on the Family, 1999. Available from http://web.archive.org/web/19991012153026/http://family.org/cforum/research/papers/a0006891.html.

Clark, Mary Ann. *Where men are wives and mothers rule: Santería ritual practices and their gender implications*. Gainesville: University Press of Florida, 2005.

Cobb, Michael L. *God hates fags: The rhetorics of religious violence*. New York: New York University Press, 2006.

Comiskey, Andrew. *How Jesus heals us through his church*. Undated. Available from http://web.archive.org/web/20021022080910/http://desertstream.org/testimonies/comiskey.htm.

Connolly, William E. The Evangelical–capitalist resonance machine. *Political Theory* 33, no. 6 (2005): 869–886.

Cooper, Darien. *You can be the wife of a happy husband*. Wheaton, Ill.: Victor, 1974.

Cossins, Anne. *Masculinities, sexualities, and child sexual abuse*. Boston: Kluwer Law International, 2000.

Cott, Nancy F. *Public vows: A history of marriage and the nation*. Cambridge, Mass.: Harvard University Press, 2000.

Dailey, Jane. Sex, segregation, and the sacred after *Brown*. *Journal of American History* 91 (2004): 119–144.

Davey, Kate. Outing whiteness: A feminist/lesbian project. In *Whiteness: A critical reader*, ed. Mike Hill, 204–225. New York: New York University Press, 1997.

Diamond, Sara. *Not by politics alone: The enduring influence of the Christian right*. New York: Guilford, 1998.

Dobson, James. *Bringing up boys*. Wheaton, Ill.: Tyndale House, 2001.

———. *Complete marriage and family home reference guide*. Wheaton, Ill.: Tyndale House, 2000.

———. Dr. Dobson's study, excerpts from *Complete marriage and family home reference guide*. Focus on the Family, 2002. Available from http://web.archive.org/web/20020314053037/http://www.family.org/docstudy/solid/a0015082.html.

———. Dr. Dobson's study, excerpts from *Complete marriage and family home reference guide*, letter to a gay man. Focus on the Family, 2001. Available from http://web.archive.org/web/20010628112319/http://www.family.org/docstudy/solid/a0015088.html.

———. Dr. Dobson's study, excerpts from *Complete marriage and family home reference guide*, origins of homosexuality. Focus on the Family, 2000. Available from http://web.archive.org/web/20010331091626/http://www.family.org/docstudy/solid/a0015082.html.

———. Dr. Dobson's study, excerpts from *Complete marriage and family home reference guide*, stable society. Focus on the Family, 2003. Available from http://web.archive.org/web/20030221040012/http://www.family.org/docstudy/solid/a0003519.html.

———. Dr. Dobson's study, February 2000. Focus on the Family, 2000. Available from http://web.archive.org/web/20000229181141/http://www.family.org/docstudy/newsletters/a0009515.html.

———. Dr. Dobson's study, June 1998. Focus on the Family, 1998. Available from http://web.archive.org/web/19981205141437/http://www.family.org/docstudy/newsletters/a0001935.html.

———. Dr. Dobson's study, June 2002. Focus on the Family, 2002. Available from http://www2.focusonthefamily.com/docstudy/newsletters/a000000264.cfm.

———. Dr. Dobson's study, November, 1998. Focus on the Family, 1998. Available from http://web.archive.org/web/19990128024529/http://www.family.org/docstudy/newsletters/a0003274.html.

———. In defending marriage—take the offensive. Focus on the Family, 2004. Available from http://web.archive.org/web/20070208041751/http://www.focusonthefamily.com/docstudy/newsletters/A000000334.cfm.

———. *Marriage under fire: Why we must win this battle*. Sisters, Ore.: Multnomah, 2004.

———. *Straight talk: What men need to know. What women should understand*. Dallas, Tex.: Word Pub Group, 1991.

———. To the husbands of Christian homemakers. Focus on the Family, 2002. Available from http://web.archive.org/web/20020307012938/http://www.family.org/married/comm/a0019596.cfm.

———. *Troubled with: Homosexuality*. Focus on the Family, 2008. Available from http://web.archive.org/web/20080203204700/http://www.troubledwith.com/LoveandSex/A000001001.cfm?topic=love+and+sex:+homosexuality.

———. *What wives wish their husbands knew about women*. Wheaton, Ill.: Tyndale House, 1975.

Echols, Alice. Cultural feminism: Feminist capitalism and the anti-pornography movement. *Social Text* 7 (Spring–Summer 1983): 34–53.

Eco, Umberto. *Six walks in the fictional woods*. Cambridge, Mass.: Harvard University Press, 1994.

Eickelman, Dale F. and James P. Piscatori. *Muslim politics*. Princeton Studies in Muslim Politics. Princeton, N.J.: Princeton University Press, 1996.

Eisenstadt, Samuel N. The transformations of the religious dimensions in the constitution of contemporary modernities: The contemporary religious sphere in the context of multiple modernities. In *Religion im kulturellen Diskurs: Festschrift für Hans G. Kippenberg zu seinem 65. Geburtstag = Religion in cultural discourse: Essays in honor of Hans G. Kippenberg on the occasion of his 65th birthday*, ed. Hans G. Kippenberg, Brigitte Luchesi, and Kocku von Stuckrad, 337–355. Berlin: W. de Gruyter, 2004.

Fausto-Sterling, Anne. *Sexing the body: Gender politics and the construction of sexuality*. New York: Basic Books, 2000.

Feldblum, Chai. The limitations of liberal neutrality arguments in favor of same-sex marriage. In *Legal recognition of same-sex partnerships: A study of national, European and international law*, ed. Mads Tønnesson Andenæs and Robert Wintemute, 55–74. Portland, Ore.: Hart, 2001.

Focus on the Family. *Husbands & wives: Homosexuality*. Focus on the Family, 2003. Available from http://web.archive.org/web/20030402084633/http://www.family.org/married/topics/a0025114.cfm.

———. Our mission, vision and guiding principles. Focus on the Family, 2007. Available from http://www.focusonthefamily.com/aboutus/A000000408. cfm.

Foucault, Michel, Collège de France, François Ewald, Alessandro Fontana, Mauro Bertani, and Association pour le Centre Michel Foucault. *"Il faut défendre la société": Cours au Collège de France (1975–1976) hautes études.* Paris: Seuil, 1997.

Frank, Thomas. *What is the matter with Kansas? How conservatives won the heart of America.* New York: Metropolitan Books, 2004.

Gallagher, Sally K. *Evangelical identity and gendered family life.* New Brunswick, N.J.: Rutgers University Press, 2003.

———. Where are the antifeminist Evangelicals? Evangelical identity, subcultural location, and attitudes toward feminism. *Gender and Society* 18, no. 4 (2004): 451–472.

Gallup Europe, EOS. Public opinion and same-sex unions. Gallup Europe, 2003. Available from http://www.ilga-europe.org/europe/issues/marriage_and_ partnership/public_opinion_and_same_sex_unions_2003.

The gay marriage debate. *Brio* magazine, 2004. Available at http://web.archive.org/ web/20040203230220/http://www.briomag.com/briomagazine/spiritual health/a0005053.html.

Geertz, Clifford. *The interpretation of cultures: Selected essays.* 2000 ed. New York: Basic Books, 1973.

Giroux, Henry A. Racial politics and the pedagogy of whiteness. In *Whiteness: A critical reader*, ed. Mike Hill, 294–315. New York: New York University Press, 1997.

Glaeser, Edward L. and Bryce A. Ward. *Myths and realities of American political geography.* Cambridge, Mass.: Harvard Institute of Economic Research, 2006. Available from http://post.economics.harvard.edu/hier/2006papers/2006list .html.

Greeley, Andrew M. and Michael Hout. *The truth about conservative Christians: What they think and what they believe.* Chicago: University of Chicago Press, 2006.

Green, J., M. Rozell and C. Wilcox. Social movement and party politics. The case of the Christian right. *Journal for the Scientific Study of Religion* 40, no. 3 (2001): 413–426.

Greenberg, Steven. *Wrestling with God and men: Homosexuality in the Jewish tradition.* Madison: University of Wisconsin Press, 2004.

Greenhouse, Linda. The Supreme Court: Texas law; Court appears ready to reverse a sodomy law. *New York Times*, March 27, 2003.

Griffith, R. Marie. *God's daughters: Evangelical women and the power of submission*. Berkeley: University of California Press, 1997.

Groothuis, Rebecca Merrill. *Good news for women: A biblical picture of gender equality*. Grand Rapids, Mich.: Baker, 1997.

Hallisey, Charles. Roads taken and not taken in the study of Theravada Buddhism. In *Curators of the Buddha: The study of Buddhism under colonialism*, ed. Donald S. Lopez, 31–62. Chicago: University of Chicago Press, 1995.

Hannerz, Ulf. *Cultural complexity: Studies in the social organization of meaning*. New York: Columbia University Press, 1992.

Harding, Susan Friend. *The book of Jerry Falwell: Fundamentalist language and politics*. Princeton, N.J.: Princeton University Press, 2000.

——. Convicted by the Holy Spirit: The rhetoric of fundamentalist Baptist conversion. *American Ethnologist* 14 (February 1987): 167–181.

Harvey, Linda. *A checklist to assess your school's risk for encouraging homosexuality 2002*. Available from http://web.archive.org/web/20030219101924/www.family.org/cforum/tempforum/A0015282.html.

Hendershot, Heather. *Shaking the world for Jesus: Media and conservative Evangelical culture*. Chicago: University of Chicago Press, 2004.

Herman, Didi. *The antigay agenda: Orthodox vision and the Christian right*. Chicago: University of Chicago Press, 1997.

——. "Then I saw a new Heaven and a new Earth": Thoughts on the Christian right and the problem of "backlash." In *Dangerous territories: Struggles for difference and equality in education*, ed. Leslie G. Roman and Linda Eyre, 63–74. New York: Routledge, 1997.

Higginbotham, Evelyn Brooks. *Righteous discontent: The women's movement in the black Baptist church, 1880–1920*. Cambridge, Mass.: Harvard University Press, 1993.

Holsinger, James. *Pathophysiology of male homosexuality*. Prepared for the Committee to Study Homosexuality of the United Methodist Church, 1991.

Hunter, James Davison. *American Evangelicalism: Conservative religion and the quandary of modernity*. New Brunswick, N.J.: Rutgers University Press, 1983.

——. *Before the shooting begins: Searching for democracy in America's culture war*. New York: Free Press; Toronto: Maxwell Macmillan Canada; Maxwell Macmillan International, 1994.

——. *Culture wars: The struggle to define America*. New York: Basic Books, 1991.

———. The enduring culture war. In *Is there a culture war? A dialogue on values and American public life*, ed. James Davison Hunter and Alan Wolfe, xii. Washington, D.C.: Pew Research Center, Brookings Institution Press, 2006.

Jäger, Sigfried. Diskurs und Wissen: Theoretische und methodische Aspekte einer kritischen Diskurs- und Dispositivanalyse. In *Handbuch sozialwissenschaftliche Diskursanalyse. Band 1: Theorien und Methoden*, ed. Reiner Keller, 81–112. Opladen, Germany: Leske + Budrich, 2001.

Jakobsen, Janet R. and Ann Pellegrini. *Love the sin: Sexual regulation and the limits of religious tolerance*. New York: New York University Press, 2003.

Jamison, Heather. Pursuing holiness in marriage (Part 3 of 3). *Reclaiming Intimacy*, 2003. Available from http://web.archive.org/web/20040623021512/http://www.family.org/married/romance/a0019336.cfm.

Johnson, William Stacy. *A time to embrace: Same-gender relationships in religion, law, and politics*. Grand Rapids, Mich.: William B. Eerdmans, 2006.

Jordahl, Steve. *New hate crime stats released*. Focus on the Family, 2002. Available from http://web.archive.org/web/20021217013752/http://www.family.org/cforum/fnif/news/a0023536.html.

Jordan, Lara Jakes. Excerpt from Santorum interview Washington. *USA Today*, 2003. Available from http://www.usatoday.com/news/washington/2003-04-23-santorum-excerpt_x.htm.

Jordan, Mark D. *Blessing same-sex unions: The perils of queer romance and the confusions of Christian marriage*. Chicago: University of Chicago Press, 2005.

———. *The ethics of sex: New dimensions to religious ethics*. Malden, Mass.: Blackwell, 2001.

Kaufman, Matt. *Gay Culture 101*. Focus on the Family, 2000. Available from http://web.archive.org/web/20050407223838/http://www.boundless.org/2000/regulars/kaufman/a0000266.html.

———. *Not afraid to come out. A celebration of freedom from homosexuality*. Focus on the Family, 1998. Available from http://web.archive.org/web/20050407191114/http://www.boundless.org/1999/features/a0000026.html.

Kimmel, Michael. Masculinity as homophobia: Fear, shame, and silence in the construction of gender identity. In *Theorizing masculinities*, ed. Harry Brod, Michael Kaufman, and Men's Studies Association (U.S.), 119–141. Thousand Oaks, Calif.: Sage, 1994.

Kimmel, Michael and Michael A. Messner, eds. *Men's lives*. Boston: Allyn and Bacon, 1995.

Koerner, Heather. The temptation to fudge. *Boundless*, 2006. Available from http://web.archive.org/web/20071011072613/http://www.boundless.org/2005/articles/a0001242.cfm.

Kroeger, Catherine Clark and Nancy Nason-Clark. *No place for abuse: Biblical & practical resources to counteract domestic violence.* Downers Grove, Ill.: Inter-Varsity Press, 2001.

LaHaye, Beverly. *The spirit controlled woman.* Eugene, Ore.: Harvest House, 1976.

Laqueur, Thomas Walter. *Making sex: Body and gender from the Greeks to Freud.* Cambridge, Mass.: Harvard University Press, 1990.

Lieber, Francis. The Mormons: Shall Utah be admitted into the union? *Putnam's Monthly* 5 (March 1855): 225–235.

Lynd, Robert Staughton and Helen Merrell Lynd. *Middletown: A study in contemporary American culture.* London: Constable, 1929.

MacKinnon, Catharine A. *Toward a feminist theory of the state.* Cambridge, Mass.: Harvard University Press, 1989.

Marx, Karl. *The Eighteenth Brumaire of Louis Bonaparte. With explanatory notes.* New York: International Publishers, 1987.

McClintock, Anne. *Imperial leather: Race, gender, and sexuality in the colonial conquest.* London: Routledge, 1995.

McGinn, Bernard. *The growth of mysticism: Gregory the Great through the 12th century.* Vol. 2: *The presence of God: A history of Western Christian mysticism.* New York: Crossroad, 1994.

Mendinger, Alan. He healed my marriage. Stonewall Revisited, 2002. Available from http://web.archive.org/web/20060527085045/http://stonewallrevisited.com/pages/alan_m.html.

Messner, Michael A. Masculinities and athletic careers. In *The social construction of gender,* ed. J. Lorber and S. A. Farrell, 66–75. Newbury Park, Calif.: Sage, 1991.

Moon, Dawne. *God, sex, and politics: Homosexuality and everyday theologies.* Chicago: University of Chicago Press, 2004.

Mosse, George L. *Nationalism and sexuality: Respectability and abnormal sexuality in modern Europe.* New York: H. Fertig, 1985.

Nagel, Joane. Masculinity and nationalism: Gender and sexuality in the making of nations. In *Nations and nationalism: A reader,* ed. Philip Spencer and Howard Wollman, 110–130. New Brunswick, N.J.: Rutgers University Press, 2005.

Nicolosi, Joseph. *Is this really good for kids?* Focus on the Family, 2002. Available from http://web.archive.org/web/20040406045344/www.family.org/cforum/teachersmag/features/a0013018.cfm.

Oakeshott, Michael Joseph and Timothy Fuller. *Religion, politics, and the moral life.* New Haven, Conn.: Yale University Press, 1993.

Omartian, Stormie. How husbands handle submission. Focus on the Family, 2003. Available from http://www.safamily.org.za/articles_marriedcouples?mode=content&id=28357&refto=3590&PHPSESSID=3ef3eba615940c883d78ff24d914792a.

Orsi, Robert A. *The Madonna of 115th Street: Faith and community in Italian Harlem, 1880–1950.* New Haven, Conn.: Yale University Press, 1985.

Paulk, Anne. Former lesbian. Stonewall Revisited, 2002. Available from http://web.archive.org/web/20050909211912/http://www.stonewallrevisited.com/pages/anne.html.

Paulk, Anne and John Paulk. The other way out. Stonewall Revisited, 2002. Available from http://web.archive.org/web/20080125075136/http://www.stonewallrevisited.com/pages/otherway.html.

Pew Research Center for the People and the Press. Most want middle ground on abortion: Pragmatic Americans liberal and conservative on social issues. Pew Research Center for the People and the Press, 2006. Available from http://people-press.org/reports/display.php3?ReportID=283.

———. *Religious beliefs underpin opposition to homosexuality.* Pew Research Center press release, 2003.

Phillips, D. Z. *Faith and philosophical enquiry.* London: Routledge & Kegan Paul, 1970.

Phillips, Kevin P. *American theocracy: The peril and politics of radical religion, oil, and borrowed money in the 21st century.* New York: Viking, 2006.

Plaskow, Judith. *Standing again at Sinai: Judaism from a feminist perspective.* New York: Harper & Row, 1990.

Pollack, William S. *Real boys: Rescuing our sons from the myths of boyhood.* New York: Random House, 1998.

Posner, Richard A. *Law, pragmatism, and democracy.* Cambridge, Mass.: Harvard University Press, 2003.

Rae, Kimberly. Does Christianity support the oppression of women? *Brio,* 2004. Available from http://web.archive.org/web/20061112090958/http://www.briomag.com/briomagazine/briobeyond/a0005335.html.

Rogers, Eugene F. *Sexuality and the Christian body: Their way into the triune God.* Challenges in Contemporary Theology. Malden, Mass.: Blackwell, 1999.

Ross, Michael. Hey Mike: Don't be controlled by lust. *Breakaway*, 2002. Available from http://web.archive.org/web/20050307072225/http://www.family.org/teenguys/breakmag/departments/a0020137.html.

———. What should I do about masturbation? Focus on the Family, 2002. Available from http://www.breakawaymag.com/HeyMike/A000000342.cfm.

Roy, Olivier. *Globalized Islam: The search for a new ummah.* New York: Columbia University Press; Paris: Centre d'Etudes et de Recherches Internationales, 2004.

Ryan, Dana. Please open my door. *Boundless*, 2002. Available from http://web.archive.org/web/20071023133344/http://www.boundless.org/2002_2003/departments/isms/a0000668.html.

Shea, William M. *The lion and the lamb: Evangelicals and Catholics in America.* Oxford: Oxford University Press, 2004.

Shellenberger, Susi. Dear Susi: Privacy and dealing with guys. *Brio*, 1998. Available from http://web.archive.org/web/20050420042830/http://www.briomag.com/briomagazine/dearsusie/a0000952.html.

———. Heaven, Christ-centered relationships and marriage. *Brio*, 2004. Available from http://web.archive.org/web/20061112091347/http://www.briomag.com/briomagazine/dearsusie/a0005691.html.

Smith, Christian. *Christian America? What Evangelicals really want.* Berkeley: University of California Press, 2000.

Smith, Michael G. *Language and power in the creation of the USSR, 1917–1953.* Contributions to the Sociology of Language, no. 80. Berlin: Mouton de Gruyter, 1998.

Sprigg, Peter. Questions and answers: What's wrong with letting same-sex couples "marry"? Family Research Council, 2006. Available from http://web.archive.org/web/20040209123725/http://www.frc.org/get.cfm?i=IF03H01&f=PG03I03.

Sprigg, Peter and Timothy Dailey, eds. *Getting it straight: What the research shows about homosexuality.* Washington, D.C.: Family Research Council, 2004.

Stanton, Glenn. Is marriage in jeopardy? Part II. Focus on the Family, undated. Available from http://www.focusonthefamily.ca/tfn/family/PDF/Marriage_in_Jeopardy.pdf.

———. What's the deal with same-sex marriage? What do you think? What does God think? *Breakaway*, 2004. Available from http://web.archive.org/web/

20060103233246/http://www.breakawaymag.com/AllTheRest/A000000091. cfm.

Stewart, Shannon Kristi. Signs of an abusive relationship. *Brio*, 2004. Available from http://web.archive.org/web/20060323124411/http://www.briomag.com/bri omagazine/briobeyond/a0005213.html.

Stoler, Ann Laura. *Carnal knowledge and imperial power: Race and the intimate in colonial rule.* Berkeley: University of California Press, 2002.

Swift, Michael. The gay manifesto. Available from http://web.archive.org/web/ 20060518122032/http://rainbowallianceopenfaith.homestead.com/Gay AgendaSwiftText.html.

Tambiah, Stanley Jeyaraja. *Buddhism betrayed? Religion, politics, and violence in Sri Lanka.* A Monograph of the World Institute for Development Economics Research (Wider) of the United Nations University. Chicago: University of Chicago Press, 1992.

Thurma, Scott. Negotiating a religious identity: The case of the gay Evangelicals. *Sociological Analysis* 52, no. 4 (1991): 333–347.

Toalston, Art. Amid a culture that has left many families frayed and others battered, James Dobson has stood strong. Nashville, Tenn.: Baptist Press, 2002. Available from 4/12/2009 http://www.bpnews.net/bpnews.asp?id=13945.

Touré. "Dirty pretty things: Review of *Restless little virgins. Love, sex, and survival at a New England prep school.* By Abigail Jones and Marissa Miley. *New York Times,* September 16, 2007.

United States Congress. "Congressional Record—House." H7480–H7506, 1996.

———. "Congressional Record—Senate." cr09se96S, S10067–S10068, 1996a.

———. "Congressional Record—Senate." cr10se96S, S10100–S10125, 1996b.

Utvik, Bjørn Olav. The modernizing force of Islam. In *Modernizing Islam: Religion in the public sphere in the Middle East and Europe,* ed. John L. Esposito and François Burgat, 43–68. London: Hurst, 2003.

Viefhues, Ludger. "On my bed at night I sought him whom my heart loves": Reflections on trust, horror, G*d, and the queer body in vowed religious life. *Modern Theology* 17, no. 4 (2001): 413–425.

Viefhues-Bailey, Ludger. *Beyond the philosopher's fear: A Cavellian reading of gender, origin, and religion in modern skepticism.* Aldershot, England: Ashgate Press, 2007.

Watters, Candice Z. "BA: Silent in church. *Boundless,* 2007. Available from http:// www.boundless.org/2005/answers/a0001459.cfm.

Wittgenstein, Ludwig and G. E. M. Anscombe. *Philosophical investigations: The German text, with a revised English translation*. 3rd ed. Oxford: Blackwell, 2001.

Wittgenstein, Ludwig, G. E. M. Anscombe, and G. H. von Wright. *On certainty*. Oxford: Blackwell, 1969.

Wolfe, Alan. The culture war that never came. In *Is there a culture war? A dialogue on values and American public life*, ed. James Davison Hunter and Alan Wolfe, 41–73. Washington, D.C.: Pew Research Center, Brookings Institution Press, 2006.

——. Response. In *Is there a culture war? A dialogue on values and American public life*, ed. James Davison Hunter and Alan Wolfe, 97–107. Washington, D.C.: Pew Research Center, Brookings Institution Press, 2006.

Wuthnow, Robert. *The restructuring of American religion: Society and faith since World War II*. Studies in Church and State. Princeton, N.J.: Princeton University Press, 1988.

INDEX